BE READY ON RACE DAY

How to Create a Custom Training Plan for Your Next Marathon or Half Marathon

Denny Krahe

Let's Tell Your Story Publishing
London

█ COPYRIGHT

Title: Be Ready On Race Day - How to Create a Custom Training Plan for Your Next Marathon or Half Marathon

First published in 2018.

Publisher: Let's Tell Your Story, 5 Century Court. Tolpits Lane, Watford, WD18 9RS

ISBN 978-1-910600-19-1

Book design: Elizabeth Hults   Editor: Rebekah Krahe

This guide is not endorsed by or affiliated with any one person or any other website or organization mentioned in this book in any way.

COPYRIGHT ACKNOWLEDGEMENTS

For every runner that has had enough of the
"one-size-fits-all" training plan...

CONTENTS

ACKNOWLEDGEMENTS

This book may have my name on the byline, but this was a team effort. Point blank, without the following people, this book does not exist.

Dan Meredith: Thanks for being the mentor I've been looking for for quite some time. Your no nonsense approach, to put it mildly, has been just what I've needed to help me take the appropriate action and get shit done. Thank you.

Colette Mason: When this book was still in its infancy, you offered to be my lifeline and to help me see this project to completion. It's taken a bit longer than I'd hoped, but without you, there's no telling how much longer it would have taken! Thanks for helping me keep my head above the water.

Elizabeth Hults: If anyone judges this book by its cover, I'll be in good shape! Thanks for putting the icing on the cake for me.

Adison Marie: You make me smile every day. Thanks for letting me have the honor of being your daddy.

Beks: Where to begin? You're my editor, my sounding board, my rock, my partner, and my best friend. Not sure I can ever repay you for everything you've done for our family, but rest assured I'll never stop trying. I love you.

ABOUT THE AUTHOR

Before we go much further, I think it would be prudent to let you know a bit more about who I am and why I'm qualified to write this book.

But first, let me tell you a couple of things that I'm not.

I'm not an elite runner.

Far from it, in fact. My current PRs are 4:08 in the marathon and 1:45 in the half. That's fast enough to put me squarely mid-pack in just about every race I've ever run, no matter the size of the field.

I'm also not an RRCA certified running coach.

I've looked into the program and decided it wasn't for me. Why? After looking through the information online, I realized that the topics and subjects covered in the two-day certification class were almost identical to the courses I took over six years of college and graduate school where I studied exercise science and sports medicine.

So why am I qualified to write this book?

Well, in large part because I'm not an elite runner and because I'm not an RRCA certified coach.

I have been a Certified Athletic Trainer (ATC) since 2004 and a Certified Strength and Conditioning Specialist (CSCS) since 2007, and you don't find many running coaches with that level of understanding of the science of sports injuries, kinesiology, and exercise science.

I don't mean to sound like a complete douche, but I know a few things about how the body works when training for and running long distances. I also feel like being a "regular" runner helps me with writing this book because I've likely been in your shoes. I've seen in my training how having a custom training plan has lead to improved race performances in both the half and full marathon.

So instead of writing with the perspective of the elites, for whom 7-minute miles is considered an "easy" pace, I'm writing this as your running equal. I know the struggle of balancing my training, family time, work responsibilities, and everything else that is going on in life at any given moment.

Other things about me that you may find interesting include:

- Big running goal: qualify for Boston.
- Second big goal: run a marathon in every state.
- Keynote speaker.
- Podcast host: Diz Runs Radio.
- Most important titles: husband to Rebekah and daddy to Adison.

Want to know anything else about me? Or are you curious for more details? Drop me a line at diz@dizruns.com, and I'll tell you more about me than you probably ever wanted to know!

Denny
February 2018
Lakeland, FL

INTRODUCTION

Is this book for you?

Maybe.

I'm not delusional enough to think that I could write a book about creating the training plan for your next marathon or half marathon and believe that it should be required reading for every amateur distance runner in the world.

That would just be silly.

That said, if any of the following statements describe you, then you would most likely benefit from knowing how to write, tweak, and adjust your training plan. Because let's be honest, those one-size-fits-all training plans? They are straight garbage.

Do you:

- Have a specific time goal you'd like to hit for your next race?
- Worry about the possibility of becoming injured while training?
- Want to structure your training intelligently and increase your mileage appropriately over the course of your training cycle?
- Enjoy having a structure in your running life?
- Know how to adjust your training schedule appropriately when life happens?

If you resonate with any of these points, then this book is something you might want to consider.

If you identify with two or three of them, then this book will help you.

If you're a little creeped out because I'm talking directly to you with each of those statements, then you've got the book you need in your hands.

Now, the ball is in your court.

You can keep training the way that you've been training in the past and keep getting the same or similar results, or you can dive in and learn the ins and outs of creating a training plan for an audience of one: you.

The choice is yours.

WHY I WROTE THIS BOOK

Why am I writing this book?

Simple! I want to be a bajillionaire, and we all know that the quickest way to earning a bajillion dollars is to write a book, right?

Wait, writing a book isn't the secret of infinite wealth and notoriety?

Well, in that case, I'm writing this book for one reason...

I HATE ONE-SIZE-FITS-ALL TRAINING PLANS

We are not one-size-fits-all humans. We are not one-size-fits-all runners. So why in the name of everything holy would we ever think that one-size-fits-all training plans would work?

Point blank, they don't.

To be fair, a one-size-fits-all training plan can help you get from the starting line of a race to the finish line of a race.

But do you know where a one-size-fits-all training plan is probably going to miss the mark?

- Helping you nail your specific time goal.
- Helping you know what to do when you develop an odd ache/pain during the training cycle.
- Helping you know how to intelligently/appropriately ramp up *your* training based on how *you* are feeling.
- Helping you tweak/adjust your training based on the unpredictability that is your life.
- Helping you create a structured plan that fits your life instead of forcing your life to try and fit into a structured plan.

Why am I writing this book?

- Because I know how important that your time goal is to you, and I want you to nail it!
- Because I know how much it sucks to be injured, and I want to help you avoid injury if possible.

- Because I know how much more efficient it is to train smarter and not harder when it comes to increasing your mileage and intensity during a training cycle.
- Because I know that life is going to happen, and knowing how to adjust your training on the fly is something you're more than likely going to have to do during a 16+ week training cycle.
- To show you that it's easier to make your training plan fit your life than to try to make your life fit your training. Always.

I'm writing this book because I want to help you be successful on race day.

And because I know, beyond the shadow of a doubt, that success on race day starts with a plan that is yours and yours alone.

WHAT WE'LL COVER

Here is a quick look at what we'll be discussing in this book.

BEFORE YOU BEGIN

I've learned many valuable lessons while writing out training plans for my clients in the past.

Feel free to learn from my mistakes instead of learning those same lessons through trial and error, as I have done.

PRE-PLAN PLAN

Before you start your training, you need to take an honest look at several factors that will impact the creation of your plan and your goals.

Have you been running regularly for the past few months or years? How many miles are you running per week? How many days can you realistically commit to training per week? And on those days, how much time do you have available to run?

There are no right or wrong answers to any of these questions, but it's important to know from where you are starting to know how to proceed with your training.

THE BASICS

At their core, all training plans contain the same structure and follow a predictable pattern.

By understanding the basic structure of your training plan, you'll be better able to customize your training to suit your needs while ensuring that you are progressing at the appropriate rate to be ready to go on the day of your race.

WORKOUT VARIETY

Training for a half or full marathon requires more than just running.

There are several different types of running workouts that, depending on your current level of fitness, you should include in your training for your race. Each type of workout serves a different purpose, and therefore, each is important for a different reason.

Once you know the different types of running workouts to include in your training, you'll want to know how to organize your training for maximum efficiency while decreasing the risk of injury as much as possible.

PRE-HAB

While training for your race, it's easy to get laser-focused on your running and lose sight of some of the little things you should be doing to keep your body from breaking down while you're gearing up for your race.

Many running injuries are preventable, provided you stay on top of the little things.

Developing, and implementing, a good pre-hab routine will go a long way toward making sure you get to the start of your race without any random aches or pains.

ADJUST ON THE FLY

Let's face it, life is nothing if not unpredictable!

I don't care if you're preparing to race at the Olympics or preparing for your first half marathon, there will be occasions (and probably several) during your training cycle where life is going to get crazy, and you're going to have to adjust your training.

When the shit hits the fan, what should you do? Skip the workout altogether? Push everything back a day to stay on track? Do a double to make up for it?

Maybe.

FINAL PREPARATIONS

In addition to planning your training, it's also important to plan for your actual race.

Taking some time to reflect upon your training, review the specifics of the course, and develop a specific strategy for the race are important steps to make sure you're as mentally prepared as you are physically.

POST-RACE RECOVERY

Just because you finish your race, it doesn't mean your training plan is over!

Decide what your recovery plan is going to look like before you run your race, and make sure you stick with it no matter what happens on race day!

WHEN TO START TRAINING

Appropriately training for an endurance event takes time.

There are a few folks that can jump off of the couch and into a race with only a week's notice, but since you're reading this, I highly doubt that you're one of them.

As a rule of thumb, give yourself about 16 weeks to properly train for your race.

Depending on your fitness level, how long you've been running consistently, and what your goals are you may adjust that time-line a bit up or down, but 16 weeks is a good estimate for the amount of time that you'll need to prepare for your race.

WHO IS THIS BOOK FOR

This book is for runners who understand that one-size-fits-all training plans truly don't fit all, and rarely even fit one.

Ultimately, this book is for:

RUNNERS WITH SPECIFIC TIME GOALS

Whatever your time goal may be, from avoiding the sweeper to qualifying for Boston, if you have a time goal you will benefit from this book.

I've heard it said that a goal without a plan is just a dream. If you have a specific time goal, having a customized plan is in-valuable.

RUNNERS WORRIED ABOUT INJURIES

No runner wants to get injured. Yet, according to multiple studies, approximately 50% of runners find themselves sidelined due to running related injuries each year.

Injuries are an inherent risk to those of us that run. That said, certain things can be done to dramatically decrease the risk of developing injuries during a training cycle and a running career.

RUNNERS WHO DESIRE STRUCTURE

Structure is a good thing.

A solid structure to your training plan will help you to stay on track while intelligently increasing the volume and intensity of your workouts over time.

A big part of reducing the risk of injury during your training cycle is a well-structured training plan that progresses you appropriately.

Ramping up your training too quickly is like playing with fire. You might get away with it once, but eventually, you'll get burned.

RUNNERS WITH BUSY LIVES

Running is something we do for fun; something that brings us joy. But we all have other things in our lives (work, family, friends, social obligations, etc.) that can, and often do, throw a wrench into our training.

This book will help you to know what to do when you are forced to miss a run for any number of reasons.

WHAT YOU WILL LEARN FROM THIS BOOK

There are three things that you are going to fully understand by the time you finish this book that will make sure you're ready when race day gets here.

HOW TO ORGANIZE A PROPER TRAINING PLAN

If you think you will be ready on race day after flying by the seat of your pants during your training cycle, you're going to be disappointed.

A good training plan is a blend of art and science. Some days, it's a little more art. Some days, it's a little more science.

Blending art and science can be chaotic at times, but having a structure in place helps the chaos stay organized.

And please note, having a structure within your training plan doesn't mean there isn't room to adjust your training schedule as needed.

More on that in a minute.

WHY VARIETY IN TRAINING IS IMPORTANT

There are several different types of running workouts, and a well-designed training plan incorporates most of them into the mix.

If you're training for a marathon, you may not think there is much benefit to doing quarter mile repeats at 85-90% intensity.

But there is.

Inevitably, you'll find some workouts you prefer more than others, but it is good for you to make sure that you incorporate all of the different options into your training plan occasionally.

Not sure what the options are other than running?

Don't worry. I'll break them all down for you.

I just want you to know from the get-go that not all runs are the same, and if you want to get the most from your training (and from this book), you're going to need to include a pinch of this and a sprinkle of that into your training mixture.

Variety is the spice of life, you know?

And that little pearl of wisdom applies as much to your running as it does to every other area of life as well.

HOW TO ADJUST YOUR TRAINING AND STILL REACH YOUR GOALS

If there is one thing we can expect in life, it is the unexpected.

If it's not one thing, it's another, am I right? You have so much on your plate from work demands, to familial obligations, to social functions, to this, that, and the other.

And now you're going to add training for a race to the mix?

Let's level for a minute. Training for your race is going to eat up a chunk of your time each week, but no single run on your schedule is ever do or die.

When life happens, and I can guarantee that it will happen at least once (and probably several times) during your training cycle, you need to know how to adjust your training appropriately.

- Do you just cancel the run and not worry about making it up? Sometimes.
- Do you shift the entire plan by a day or two, so you don't miss a workout? Sometimes.
- Do you switch out the missed workout for another workout another day but keep everything else the same? Sometimes.

Remember, it's art *and* science!

And as such, there is never a cut and dry way that you should adjust your training plan when the unpredictability of life happens.

That said, there are some guidelines that I tend to follow when working with my clients to help them stay on track amidst the chaos that I'm going to share with you.

HOW TO USE THIS BOOK

This book is organized in a way that lays out everything I do, step by step, when working with a client to create a training plan for a specific race.

With that in mind, my recommendation would be to read this book once through, front to back, to get a feel for the process of creating your training plan *before* you start putting yours together.

Once you have an idea of how to tackle the creation of your training plan, you can go back through and use the book as a guide for each step along the way.

Of course, if you want to just jump ahead to the section of the book that you're struggling with, go for it! You bought the book; you use it however you want!

Just be aware that in some cases, an issue/problem that you're facing in the creation of your training plan may simply be a matter of putting your cart before your horse. By reading through the book first, you may be able to prevent said issue by changing the order of the steps that you take in the creation of your plan.

You know, like putting the cart behind the horse instead of in front of it.

MATERIALS NEEDED

The only thing you need to create your plan is a calendar, either physical or digital.

Pretty much all spreadsheet software (Excel, Numbers, Google Sheets) have calendar templates that you can use and customize to your heart's content. You can also just use the native calendar app on your phone/tablet/computer or download any of the calendar apps that are available.

While I do all of my clients' training plans digitally, if I'm honest, I prefer having an actual calendar that I can look at/touch/feel for my personal training schedule. There's just something about taking pen to paper to write a plan that I don't get from sitting in front of a screen and typing the workouts into the cell of a calendar.

But honestly, whatever floats your boat is fine. Just make sure you can see at least four months into the future so you can be sure to plan your workouts accordingly.

BEFORE YOU BEGIN

When you're ready to write your training plan, here are a few suggestions that you might want to keep in mind.

DON'T WRITE MORE THAN 1-2 WEEKS AT A TIME

At some point, and probably at several points, during your training cycle life is going to get in the way and screw up your plan.

The more of your plan you write at once, the more likely something is going to get in the way that will cause you to rework your plan multiple times.

By writing only one to two weeks at a time, you save yourself from repeatedly rewriting weeks of your training.

It only took me a few instances of rewriting the majority of a training plan due to a client missing a week of workouts for one reason or another to realize that there is no need to write all 16 weeks at once.

WORK BACKWARDS FROM RACE DAY TO (TENTATIVELY) SCHEDULE LONG RUNS

While you may want to abstain from writing out the entire plan at the beginning of your training cycle, it is wise to work backward from race day to plan a gradual increase in your long run mileage.

I've had more than one instance, as a coach, where I didn't progress my client early enough in training and, we had to try and cram in too many miles over the last few weeks.

Needless to say, that is not an ideal situation.

Now I give myself a general frame of reference for where I want our long runs to be each week, which allows me to progress intelligently over the course of the entire training cycle.

ONCE PER MONTH, PLAN AN "EASY" WEEK

Part of increasing your training volume/intensity intelligently is knowing that an occasional easy week is a good thing.

To be clear, an easy week is not the same thing as an off week. It simply means that you cut the total mileage back a bit and maybe ease off the intensity of your workouts a notch or two to allow your body a little break.

When you're tentatively planning your long run progression over the course of your training cycle, make sure that you're planning a couple of weeks where you cut the mileage back.

You'll appreciate the break, both mentally and physically, I promise.

PRE-PLAN PLAN

Before you sit down and begin writing out your training plan, you need to do some pre-planning.

Why? Because getting your ducks in a row before you start the actual planning process will not only make your planning go much more smoothly, but it will also make your plan more effective in helping you reach your goal.

And that is what we are trying to do here, right? Right.

In this chapter, we will be covering:

- Self-assessment of your current fitness.
- How many days you can train.
- How much time you can commit to training.
- Looking back at the past 60 days.
- Setting a realistic goal.

If you're serious about being ready on race day, this is a part of the process that may seem trivial, but it is of vital importance.

Many runners I have worked with sign up for a race, set their goal, and then come to me for advice on how to make their goal a reality.

The problem is, they haven't taken into account what will be required of them regarding training to make their goal a reality. And sometimes I'll get into putting a client's plan together only to realize that the person hasn't been running enough before the start of the training cycle to be able to do the amount of running necessary.

If the individual had looked at those variables *before* deciding upon their goal for the race, it would make for a smoother training cycle and one less awkward conversation I'd have to have where I explain that I'm a coach and not a miracle worker.

So do yourself a favor and spend the time necessary to go through this chapter and do the pre-planning work that I have outlined for you.

Pre-planning isn't a fun chore. It isn't particularly sexy. But it puts you in a position to set yourself up for success once your training officially starts.

SELF-ASSESSMENT OF CURRENT FITNESS

Take an honest moment right now, and think about how fit you are today.

Go ahead; I'll wait.

You've got an accurate idea of your fitness now, right?

Or did you struggle with knowing where to even begin to determine your current level of fitness?

Point blank, how is your current level of fitness? Good? Fair? Could be better?

Those aren't exactly "accurate" measures of fitness, and those types of measures can be next to impossible to compare over time. And if you can't get an accurate comparison over time, how do you know if your fitness is improving?

You don't.

What we need instead is a straightforward and objective way to measure your fitness. This will give you an idea of where you are right now, and it will also become your baseline to compare back to as you progress through this training cycle and beyond.

In the past, I struggled with objectively assessing my fitness. That is why I use a simple chart that helps us take the subjective question of "how would you rate your current level of fitness" and turn it into something that you can objectively measure quickly and easily.

To get a PDF copy of this table, head to the resources page at the back of the book. And if you'd like to just mark up this page right here and right now, please be my guest!

Activity	Time
Current mile	
Current 5k	
Longest run (last 30 days)	

You don't need to have each of these data points to gauge your current level of fitness, but the more you have, the better.

FILLING OUT THE CHART

At first glance, filling out the chart with your information probably seems pretty simple.

And to a certain extent, it is.

I'm pretty sure you won't need any help figuring out how to determine your longest run in the past 30 days.

But there are a couple of things that you should keep in mind concerning the mile and 5k times to ensure that your data helps you objectively find your current level of fitness.

First of all, what does current mean? When I say current mile time and current 5k time, what is the time frame I am talking about? The more recent the better, but as long as the data is coming from the past few months, it's probably close enough.

If you haven't run an all-out mile or 5k race in the past few months, does that make this chart useless?

Nope.

You are just going to need to add a couple of time trials into your training, the sooner the better, to get the required data.

And don't worry, time trials are easy peasy.

Make sure you get in a good warm-up, one that includes some strides (short bursts of higher speed running) to elevate your heart rate and prepare your body for the time trial. Once you feel good and ready, reset your watch and go for it!

Run whichever distance you're testing as hard as you can, and note your finish time.

That is now your current time for the particular distance.

Please note: do not run a 5k time trial and use the time from your first mile as your mile time trial.

Do these tests separately, preferably a week or more apart, to get an accurate assessment of your current times.

WHAT DO YOU DO WITH THE DATA?

Write it down.

Like I said, this is now your baseline assessment of your current fitness.

As for how you'll use this information for helping you put your training plan together, this data will help you to determine a realistic goal for the race. You will also use this information to get an idea of what pace to run with specific workouts, but we will get into that a bit later.

WHICH DAYS CAN YOU TRAIN

Your life is busy. I know it is.

All of us are busy. Whether it's our running, our work, our families, our social calendar, or any number of other activities in our lives, we are often pulled in a dozen different directions every day.

That's why, in addition to honestly looking at your current level of fitness, you need to look at your current schedule and honestly determine how many days you can realistically commit to your training.

Feel free to use the chart on the next page, or head to the resources section to download a copy, to help you accurately audit your typical week so you can see just how much time you have available (or don't have available) each day.

Start filling out the chart with anything and everything that you regularly do each week that would prevent you from running during a particular time.

Grocery shopping. Work. PTA Meetings. Nothing is off limits. If you do it weekly, include it in the appropriate grid.

Don't blow this exercise off.

Believe me; it's much better to know how many days you realistically have available to train now than to be forced to face reality once you've set your goal and started working towards it.

Sun.	Mon.	Tue.	Wed.	Thur.	Fri.	Sat.

HOW MUCH TIME YOU CAN COMMIT

Now that we've looked at what days may or may not be available for your training, it's time to look at how much time is available on the days you can commit to training.

Keep in mind that minimum amount of time that needs to be set aside for a training run.

30-45 minutes most days, but a little more on the weekends? That's fine.

Only a few days per week, but those days are pretty much wide open? That works too.

Just determine the amount of time you will realistically have available for you each of the days that you can commit to running.

Don't worry about how much or how little time is available for now.

LOOK AT THE PAST 60 DAYS

How have the past two months of training been for you?

You could make a very well thought out argument that what you have been doing for the couple of months leading up to the start of your training plan is as important as anything written in your plan.

Shoot, you could make the argument that those couple of months are *more* important than what's in your training plan!

That's because the work you do before your training plan starts is what I like to call the building of your base.

If you start your training plan with a solid base, you are ready to go from day one.

That's how important your base is.

A strong base gives you something from which you can push off; something you can build upon as you progress through your training plan.

If you don't have a solid base in place before you start your training, there is a good chance that you'll need to spend the first month or more building/solidifying your base before you can start focusing on your training.

And that is not a good thing.

So take a look at your past 60+ days of training.

Have you been consistent? How many miles have you been averaging per week? What is your ratio of easy and hard runs during the past couple of months?

If you use any running apps or fitness trackers, you have no excuse for not knowing (in detail) what your training has looked like for the past two months.

Take the time to look through your data and get an idea of how firm your foundation is at the moment.

SET A REALISTIC GOAL

Finally, let's talk goal setting.

Why did we wait this long to decide upon a goal for a race?

Simple. I'm a fan of being successful.

That said, I'm not proposing setting a low bar that virtually guarantees your success.

I just don't want you to set your heart on a goal that is beyond the realm of possibility at the moment.

I've had to have conversations with my coaching clients before where I tell them that their goal simply isn't realistic at this time. Believe me, those calls are not fun.

I'm all for dreaming big, I really am.

I would encourage you to set some huge running goals for yourself and continue to chip away at them for years until you are successful.

But when you are creating your training plan for your next race, that is *not* the time to dream big.

Doing so will often lead, at best, to disappointment. And at worst, it may result in an injury that could prevent you from running for many months to come.

So before you set a goal for your race, take a good hard look at where you are right now. How is your fitness? How many days and how much time do you realistically have available to train? How solid is your base?

Then, check out the course profile on the race's website to get a general idea of how the race actually "looks." Are there some rolling hills spaced evenly over the course? Is there a huge climb in the last few miles of the race? Is the course mostly flat?

Once you've looked in depth at each of these areas, and only then, it is time to settle upon your goal for this race.

SUMMARY

There are several things you need to do before you begin the actual writing of your plan.

The tasks aren't particularly fun and they aren't particularly sexy. But they are important parts of the process of making sure that you are ready on race day.

Self-assessment of current fitness

Having an objective measure of your current fitness before you begin training is important. It also gives you something to compare during your training cycle to gauge your progress.

Three simple data points you can use to assess your fitness objectively are a current mile time, current 5k time, and longest distance run in the past month.

Which days can you train

Which days of the week can you commit to training? One of the most important factors regarding your success during a training cycle is consistently showing up for your training runs.

You can spend thousands of dollars on the best gear and hire the world's greatest running coach, but if you don't show up on the days you are supposed to be running, you'll be wasting your money.

Look at your calendar and figure out what days/times you can train and what days/times are completely out of the question.

Write it out and keep the information close. You are going to need it.

How much time you can commit

In addition to knowing which days are available, you also need to know how much time you have available on each day.

You may be surprised at how much time you have available to train on most days, especially if you realize that most runs don't need to be any longer than an hour.

Shoot, just carving out 30-45 minutes for a run is plenty on more than a few days.

Look at the past 60 days

How have your last two months of running been? Have you been consistent in your training? Sporadic at best?

In addition to assessing your current fitness, it's also important to take an overall look at how your base building has gone leading up to the start of your training cycle. The more sound your base is, the more you can push yourself in your workouts.

If you have an activity tracker or running watch, this shouldn't be particularly difficult. Upload your data and spend a little time looking through it.

Set a realistic goal

Once you have all of this pre-planning information together, it's time to set your goal for the upcoming race.

If you have regularly been running for the past couple of months and your schedule isn't too packed, aim high!

If life has been crazy lately and isn't showing any signs of slowing down, now isn't the time to be chasing a new PR or your first BQ.

Taking the time to do some pre-planning before you write your training plan is an essential component of writing a good plan.

Please, don't skip over this step on your way to writing your training plan! Because if you do, you may be setting yourself up for failure due to completely unrealistic expectations.

THE BASICS

While I'm very much against the idea of having a one-size-fits-all training plan for any runner, it would be foolish of me to suggest that there aren't similarities between most well-written training plans.

In this chapter, I'll be giving you the blueprint of how to construct your training plan in roughly 4-week blocks.

In practice, these blocks can be a little longer or a little shorter, but the phases of your training plan will ultimately be the same.

When it comes to the components of your training plan, these phases are the bones that will give your plan its shape:

- Length of training plan.
- First quarter: settle in/solidify base.
- Second quarter: ramp up.
- Third quarter: heaviest total training volume.
- Fourth quarter: peak volume, taper.

As much as I rant and rave against everything one-size-fits-all, you'd be forgiven for thinking that I'm saying that this is the one-size-fits-all skeleton of training plans.

I'm not.

This skeleton is the foundation that most training plans are built upon and from which the uniqueness of your training plan will become apparent.

Still not buying it? Think about your favorite pair of jeans for a minute.

Would you call them one-size-fits-all?

I hope not!

However, any good pair of blue jeans is going to have a few things in common: a right leg, a left leg, a zipper (not a button fly- what were they thinking!?!) and a button to secure the waist.

And it is from that basic framework that the myriad of different cuts, styles, and brands of blue jeans emerge.

It is the same with your training plan.

The different phases of your training plan are nearly universal. Knowing how to work within those phases will help you successfully customize your plan.

So let's dive in.

LENGTH OF TRAINING PLAN

Why are standard training plans 16 weeks long?

I don't fricking know!

What I do know is that there is no legitimate reason to suggest that 16 weeks is the perfect amount of time that is required to train for a half or full marathon.

That said, I can think of more than a few reasons why 16 weeks is about right.

First of all, 16 weeks is enough time to ramp up your fitness and your mileage so that your body has a chance to adapt/adjust to the demands that you are placing on it without breaking down.

And that is a magnificent thing!

16 weeks is also enough time to prepare for a race without being "too much" time.

With the race never being more than four months away, there is a sense of urgency that is present to help you stay motivated to do the necessary work.

Again, there is nothing magical about 16 weeks. If you'd like to give yourself a little more time, go for it. If you're short on time, depending on your fitness, your base, and your goals, you can still be ready to race hard in 10-12 weeks.

As we go forward, just note that I'm operating under the assumption that the training plan you are creating is 16 weeks. If your training plan is going to be a little longer or a little shorter, that's fine. Just adjust any time frames that I'm referencing accordingly.

FIRST QUARTER: SETTLE IN/ SOLIDIFY BASE

The first quarter of your training plan is all about settling into the structure of your plan and adding to your base level of fitness.

SETTLE INTO THE NEW PLAN

At the start of a new training cycle, it's important to allow yourself time to get adjusted to the new schedule/routine that you'll be following for the next few months.

Because even though you took the time to audit your routine and determine the amount of time you will realistically have to train for your race, there's a difference between making your training work on paper and making it work in real life.

So for these first few weeks, focusing on sticking with your training schedule as consistently as possible is key.

SOLIDIFY YOUR FITNESS BASE

In addition to settling into the actual structure of your training plan, the first quarter also gives you an opportunity to solidify your base level of fitness and gradually start upping your mileage.

I talk about the base level of fitness a lot, and there is a reason for that: it's important! Your base level of fitness is one of the most important buffers from an injury that you have, provided you've taken the time to make sure it's solid.

How do you solidify your base?

Consistent training with steady, but gradual, increases in volume and intensity.

Needless to say, solidifying your base level of fitness isn't exciting. It's not flashy, or sexy, or the kind of thing that you're likely to brag about on social media.

But it's important.

There's a reason why home builders take the time to lay a firm foundation before building a house. Without a good foundation, a home will be more likely to collapse under the weight of itself. It will also be less likely to weather storms without severe damage.

And it's the same thing with your running.

If you don't make sure your base of fitness is solid, the chances of your body breaking down when you crank up the volume/intensity of the plan increases. And when life happens at various points during your training cycle, you'll be less likely to miss a beat when you're forced to skip a workout or two (or a week or two) if your base of fitness is rock solid.

Now, in an ideal world, you'd start your training cycle with a solid base already in place, but not many runners do that.

So if your training hasn't officially started yet, use however much time you have left to focus on solidifying your base. Doing so will make the first quarter of your training go much more smoothly, I promise.

SECOND QUARTER: RAMP UP

In the second quarter of your training plan, you'll start cranking things up a bit. During the second quarter, both the volume and the intensity of your training will be increasing steadily week after week.

While you will be increasing your mileage in this quarter, specifically the distance of your long runs, please remember to do so gradually. The idea here is ramping up steadily, not taking the elevator.

Steady increases in your training volume are the goal for a couple of reasons.

One, it gives your body time to adapt/adjust to the increased demands, which lessens your chance of developing an injury. Making a big jump in the distance of your long run from one week to the next causes additional stress and strain on your bones, ligaments, muscles, and joints. By keeping those increases gradually consistent over this quarter, you decrease the odds that a physical breakdown will occur during the training cycle.

What constitutes a gradual increase in training volume? The rule of thumb that most running experts agree on is that you should increase your long runs by no more than 10% from one week to the next.

So if you're running 5 miles this week, you can bump next week's run up by a half of a mile (10%), and run 5.5 miles.

That said, keep in mind that this is just a rule of thumb and not some immutable law handed down from the heavens on stone tablets. Some runners will be able to handle slightly more aggressive increases; some will need to be more conservative.

The key to increasing your volume in the second quarter of your training, or at any point really, is that you listen to your body and react accordingly.

A second reason that the gradual increase in training volume is better than taking a dramatic leap forward has nothing to do with the physical challenges and everything to do with the mental ones.

By keeping your increases in mileage modest but steady, especially in the first half of your training cycle, you are setting yourself up for success. Every week of your training cycle, except your planned "recovery weeks," you are doing a little bit more. This means that every week is a win.

And we love winning.

These small wins that you accumulate on the way toward the second half of your training cycle, and the race itself, will help you to be confident in yourself when you have a run that isn't going according to plan. And believe me, you will have those days!

However, if you're trying to make larger increases in your training, you are running the risk that you will have more long runs that don't necessarily end on a positive note. While we all have bad runs from time to time, having a bad run every time you increase your distance isn't going to give you much confidence that you will be ready on race day.

If your training plan doesn't have you feeling ready and confident on the day of your race, then it has failed you.

THIRD QUARTER: HEAVIEST TOTAL TRAINING VOLUME

You've heard of the dog days of summer, yes?

Well, the third quarter of most training plans is kind of like the dog days of training cycles.

If you're increasing your running volume correctly over the entire training cycle, the third quarter is going to be the quarter with the highest number of miles run. And as such, you're likely to be tired—physically and mentally.

If you accept that fact and persevere through this quarter, you'll be in great shape on race day.

As you continue to increase the distances of your long runs during the third quarter of training, please do so intelligently. Your week-to-week increases can be slightly larger than they have been up to this point, but you still need to listen to your body and respond accordingly.

With your total volume being at its highest this quarter, you also need to make sure you are prioritizing all of the other "little things" to make sure that your body doesn't start breaking down.

Make sure you're eating well and drinking plenty of water every day. Put a premium on foam rolling, stretching, and other pre-hab exercises (more on that later).

And most importantly, make sure you're getting enough sleep at night. Remember, while you are sleeping your body is working overtime to repair tissues damaged by running and also making you stronger, so you'll be less likely to break down in the future.

Note: If you aren't getting enough sleep, you are minimizing the effects of your workouts, and you are increasing your risk of injury.

Safe to say, neither outcome is what you're striving for, eh?

FOURTH QUARTER: PEAK VOLUME, TAPER

The fourth quarter of your training cycle gives you a taste of two extremes in your training.

On one extreme, you'll likely be completing your longest run of the training cycle as well as logging your highest one-week mileage total.

But on the other hand, you'll also dramatically slash your volume in the lead-up to the race during the taper period.

PEAK MILEAGE

If you ask a dozen runners/running coaches how long the longest training run should be before a half/full marathon, you're likely to get a dozen different answers.

So clearly, there is no one-size-fits-all answer to the question of what your longest run should be before your race.

That said, there are three prominent schools of thought in which those dozen or so answers can be placed. When you're creating your training plan, you'll have to decide which camp you're in to determine how long your longest pre-race run will be.

Close, but not too close

Subscribers to the "close, but not too close" training philosophy tend to err on the side of caution when it comes to the longest run before the race.

For those running a half marathon, that usually means getting one or two runs in during the fourth quarter that are in the 9-10 mile range. And for those running a full marathon, that range is 19-20 miles.

The thought here is that those distances are close enough to what you'll be doing on race day that you will be able to finish the race, but not so much that you'll be excessively fatigued after the workout.

This philosophy, in my view, is fine for those that simply want to finish a race in one piece. If your max training runs are close enough to the distance you'll be racing, you will figure out how to cross the finish line on race day.

The downfall of "close, but not too close" in my view is that you won't know what the later stages of the race will feel like and how your body will respond. It may not sound like a big jump to go from 10 miles to 13.1, or from 20 miles to 26.2, but if you've never done it before, that can be an awful lot of uncharted territory for any runner.

The finish line is in sight

Another school of thought is to train up to a distance that brings the finish line within sight.

If you follow this training philosophy, you will end up pushing your longest run *almost* to the length of the race itself, but not quite.

So for the half, you'll probably do a run of about 11-12 miles, and 22-24 for those running a full marathon.

By running far enough that the "finish line is in sight," you'll have much less "unknown" distance to cover on race day. Knowing how your body responds when you get into those longer distances, especially in marathon training, will help you to know what you're likely to experience on race day and help you prepare for whatever may come your way.

In my opinion, most runners that want to finish their race strong need to *at least* finish their longest run pre-race with the finish line in sight. Of course, there are some exceptions here based on the total volume of training and the number of years you've been running, but if you have a goal beyond simply finishing the race, you should plan to have at least one long run that is pretty darn close to the length of your race.

Train long, race short

The third idea is a bit controversial, at least in some running circles, but it is not without merit. The idea here is to have your longest training run be *longer* than the length of the race you are running.

The reason behind this idea is simple: if you can go longer in training, you should have no problem going the distance required on race day itself. You'll know how your body responds at every stage of the race, and there will not be any point during the race where you can say "I've never run this far before."

So for those planning to race 13.1 miles, the longest training run will be 15+ miles. And for those running 26.2 who are going to train long and race short, 28+ miles before the marathon is a good target.

My thoughts on this philosophy are a bit mixed. I regularly push past 13.1 miles when I'm training for a half marathon, and I do believe that "training long and racing short" helps me on race day. I'm able to dig deep and confidently know that I have enough gas in the tank to finish the distance of the race.

But in my marathon training, I've yet (as of this writing) to go beyond 23-24 miles while training for a marathon. However, I am seriously thinking about adding an ultra or two to my training mix to see if running past 26.2 may be beneficial for me (mentally and physically) for the next time I race a full.

Whichever of these philosophies you decide to follow in preparation for your race, remember that they are each viable options.

The biggest determining factor is your goal for the race.

The more ambitious your goal is, the closer you want to get to running up to (or beyond) the length of the race you are running.

That said, don't overdo it.

The last thing you want to do is develop an injury that may prevent you from running the race entirely because you were pushing too hard in the handful of weeks before the race.

TAPER

Regardless of what you end up doing for your longest training run before your race, you'll be cutting your mileage a couple of weeks before the race to allow your body to rest and recharge before you toe the line.

The taper period, as it's called, is of vital importance and will be covered in much more depth later.

I only wanted to mention it here, as it is a major component of the fourth quarter of your training plan.

SUMMARY

While every training plan is uniquely different, they all are made up of the same components.

And each phase of your training plan has a distinct purpose in helping you to be ready on race day.

As a reminder, the building blocks that most training plans begin with are:

Length of training plan

Typically 16 weeks, though there is no reason that 16 weeks has become the magic number regarding the duration of a training cycle.

If you feel like you need more than 16 weeks to prepare for your race, give yourself a little longer. If your race is only 12-14 weeks away and you're just now getting into your training, adjust accordingly.

16 weeks has become the standard length of training plans because it is a long enough period to build your level of fitness incrementally without being so long that it feels like the day of the race will never get here. If you need to lengthen or shorten your training, that's ok.

First quarter: settle in/solidify base

The first quarter of your training plan is all about settling into what is going to be your new running/training routine for the next few months.

For some runners, the first quarter of your training plan

and your regular running routine when you're not training for a race will look very similar.

And for others, there may well be an extra day or two of running per week during the training cycle.

In either case, the first quarter of any training plan is the time for you to adjust to your training routine and make sure your base is solid so that when your training starts to pick up in the coming weeks, you'll be ready.

Second quarter: ramp up

During the second quarter of your training plan, your total volume and workout intensity start to increase.

Longer runs are getting longer. The pace during harder workouts is getting faster.

Third quarter: heaviest total training volume

The third quarter of your training plan, whether you're training for a half marathon or a full marathon, is going to have your highest total training volume of any of the quarters in your training plan.

The long runs continue to build upon each other on a near-weekly basis, and in some instances, you may even be doing training runs longer than the distance of your race.

Fourth quarter: peak volume, taper

The fourth quarter of your training cycle often includes your longest run or two of the training cycle, but it also includes a couple of weeks where you strategically pull back on your mileage to allow your legs to recover and feel fresh on race day.

And both of these pieces of the puzzle are crucial to ensuring that you will be ready on race day.

Now that you understand the basic structure of your training plan, you can begin tweaking and customizing your plan to fit your needs.

But before I turn you loose, there are a few other things we need to go over, starting with the different types of workouts you'll be choosing from to create your plan.

WORKOUT VARIETY

In the last chapter, we talked about what you need to do to create the basic structure of your training plan.

In this chapter, we will be focusing on what you need to do to flesh out your training plan and make it your own.

Training for a race, no matter the distance or the goal, requires that you do several different types of workouts to help you prepare--mentally and physically--for your race.

What does that mean?

In simple English, it means that not all runs/workouts are created equal.

Therefore, it is important to make sure that you have a variety of running workouts in your training plan.

We have a lot of ground to cover in this chapter, specifically:

- Maintain and solidify your base.
- The different types of workouts you should be doing.
- How to schedule your workouts intelligently.
- The taper period: what it is, why it's important, and why it can be the toughest part of your training cycle to follow.

Keep in mind as you're reading this chapter that there is no right way for you to train for your race.

That may sound pretty straightforward, and to some degree it is, but you'll find that from here on out things get much more abstract.

At this point, your plan becomes *yours* and no one else's.

For you to be properly ready on race day, however, you will want to include a mixture of all of the components of this chapter in your training plan.

What that mixture ultimately ends up being?

That's for you to decide.

MAINTAIN AND SOLIDIFY YOUR BASE

Ideally, you will already have a solid base of fitness before you start your training cycle.

Yeah, about that. You and I both know that the world we live in is far from ideal...

Whether or not you start your training cycle with a rock solid base of fitness, your base is one area on which you should always be working.

That means that before, during, and after your race, you need to be proactive when it comes to making sure that when a crack develops in your base, you are quick to fill it in and smooth it over.

Because if you ignore your base, you are asking for trouble down the road, often in the form of an injury.

So how do you maintain a solid base of fitness throughout your training cycle? And in an even broader sense, how do you do it over your entire running career?

Simple: you run easy.

THE DIFFERENT TYPES OF WORKOUTS

A well-designed training plan includes more than the instruction to "run." It requires a balance of the various kinds of workouts, within which is an almost endless number of options that you can employ to keep your workouts fresh for years and years.

EASY/RECOVERY RUN

The importance of easy running is often overlooked because an easy run is, by definition, easy.

And if you're not working hard, there can't be much benefit, right?

Nope.

Easy running is important for a couple of reasons.

Easy running rebuilds/solidifies/reinforces your base, pure and simple.

No matter where you are in your training cycle, it is important to maintain your base level of fitness. When you do the higher intensity workouts, you stress and strain your base. That stressing and straining is important, as that is what helps you improve your overall speed and endurance.

Easy running also helps with the recovery process after hard workouts by not stressing and straining the body as much.

So you're still able to train without breaking your body down further, thus reducing the risk of injury while improving your overall fitness.

LONG RUN

The long run is pretty self-explanatory, no?

You start running, and then you keep running for a while.

A long while.

And that's pretty much it.

Ok, there's a little more to the long run than that, but try not to overthink it.

Long runs are typically scheduled once per week, and the pacing is somewhat relaxed. Ideally, your long run pace should be at a level where you can comfortably maintain a conversation while speaking in full sentences.

VARIATIONS OF THE LONG RUN

Let's be real: long runs can get boring.

When you're in the midst of a training cycle, setting out to run at a relaxed pace for 2-3 hours can be less than exciting for runners at every level of experience.

If the long, steady-paced run is your thing, by all means, go for it! But if you'd like to add a little spice to your long runs, there are plenty of options to help you do so.

Race pace

In a race pace long run, you'll do a portion of your mileage at the speed you need to run to hit your time goal for your race. Typically, a race pace long run will include a few miles of easy running at the start and end of the workout, with the middle half or so being at race pace.

Negative split

In running, a negative split happens when you run faster over the course of the race or workout so that each segment, or split, is quicker than the one prior. A negative split on a long run typically means that you're running the second half of your distance faster than the first half.

Progression run

A progression run is similar to a negative split run, only cranked up to 11! With a negative split run, you don't need to get progressively faster each mile. You are only trying to run the second half quicker than the first. With progressive runs, at predetermined intervals, you are running progressively faster. So for example, in a progressive run you may start off at an easy pace, then pick it up to marathon goal pace, then half marathon goal pace, then 10k pace, then as hard as you can for the last mile or so. Progression runs are great workouts, but they are hard!

Easy-hard-easy

An easy-hard-easy run is what you'd expect it to be. You start out running easily. Then you run hard. Then you run easy again until you finish the workout. The simplest way to incorporate an easy-hard-easy workout into your training is to divide your total mileage for your long run by three and do the first and last third easy with the middle third being hard. But you can feel free to color outside of the lines on this one and divide your segments however you see fit.

TEMPO RUN

Tempo runs are hard.

That said, a tempo run is a very impactful training run no matter what race distance you are preparing to run.

When doing a tempo workout, you are trying to settle into a pace that is just at the high end of what you can comfortably maintain, and then hold that pace for a certain amount of time or distance.

What that means, in case you were wondering, is that if you are doing your tempo miles correctly, you are going to hurt for the majority of the workout.

And by the majority, I mean the entire thing.

But, the payoff for your suffering is substantial.

For shorter length races, a tempo run is going to help you to be able to build a strong finishing kick. Tempo workouts will help you hold on to your goal pace over the final few miles of longer distance races as well.

FINDING TEMPO PACE

Maintaining proper tempo pace for the duration of your workout is difficult, to say the least.

But figuring out what pace you should be running at isn't nearly as hard.

The number of miles that you're going to run at tempo pace will determine what pace is right for you. If you're doing 4-5 miles at tempo (or less), aim for about 15-30 seconds slower than your current 5k pace. If you're going to do more than 5 miles at tempo, add about a minute to your 5k pace.

If you did the pre-plan planning that I recommended, you should know your current 5k pace. So this shouldn't be diffi-cult to figure out at all.

Once you've determined your target pace, you're ready to go!

Tempo runs can be completed virtually anywhere, just make sure you allow yourself a mile or so to warm up before you dial it up to the appropriate pace and attempt to settle in for the hard part of your workout.

INTERVALS

Interval training, at its core, involves running at a high intensity for a set distance/time, running (or walking) at an easy pace for a set distance/time, and then rinsing and repeating the process.

Intervals are also commonly referred to as repeats since, in many cases, you are repeating the same interval over and over.

That said, there is a lot of room for including variety in your interval workouts.

Like, a whole lot.

Perhaps the most logical place to start when talking about the different varieties is in the length of the intervals: long vs. short.

LONG INTERVALS

As you probably have guessed, long intervals are long.

Thanks, Captain Obvious.

What that means is that the segment of the interval where you are running hard is longer. Anything that is going to take you five minutes or longer to complete, in my mind at least, is a long interval.

SHORT INTERVALS

If long intervals are long, I bet you can probably infer what short intervals are, eh?

Yeah, you got it.

Let's not overthink things here. If long intervals take longer than five minutes of hard running to complete, then short intervals are anything where your hard effort is less than five minutes.

Simple enough?

MORE DIFFERENCES BETWEEN LONG AND SHORT

All Captain Obvious jokes aside, there are some differences between long and short intervals that you need to be aware of before you start adding them to your training routine.

First of all, your pace.

Do not run all intervals at the same pace.

To try and keep things as simple as possible, the shorter the interval, the higher the intensity.

Please, don't try to run your quarter mile intervals and your two-mile intervals at the same pace!

When I'm explaining interval training to my coaching clients, I tell them that I want them hurting when they get to the end of the hard segment. I want them to be tired and ready for a chance to walk/catch their breath.

But, I also want them to be able to keep going for a little farther if they had to.

Make sense?

Admittedly, this is tough to do. Judging your pace so that you're pushing it almost, but not quite, to the limit each time takes a lot of practice. So if you don't get it right the first time, don't worry. The more familiar you get with the different types of intervals, the better you'll become at judging the pace required for that particular workout.

And speaking of pace, another thing that I should mention is that you really should not aim to be at a certain pace with each interval.

If you're doing your intervals correctly, there is a good chance that your intervals will get slower over the course of your workout.

And that is ok.

As fatigue builds up in your muscles, you may be running with the same amount of effort on your eighth repeat as you did on your first, but your pace per mile may be 30 to 60 seconds slower.

This is especially likely if you overcook one of your early intervals by running too hard.

If you find yourself in this scenario (and if you regularly do intervals, it's not a matter of if, but when), remember that the goal is to feel fatigued when you finish but to be able to continue if needed.

In other words, intervals are more about effort expended than speed.

THE RECOVERY PERIOD

The recovery period of interval training is critical.

As I mentioned above, in an ideal world when you finish your hard interval you are almost spent. Not quite, but almost.

Before your next hard segment, you need to be able to catch your breath and allow your muscles to recover enough that you're able to run the next hard interval.

And that is why there is a recovery period.

During the recovery period, it's ok to walk a little bit, especially right after you finish your hard interval.

You're probably gasping for breath, and your legs will be burning, so go ahead and walk for 30-60 seconds. After that, pick it up to a very easy jog for the remainder of the recovery period.

Speaking of which, how long should the recovery period be?

It depends.

If we are speaking in generics, the longer the hard effort, the longer the recovery period should be.

Upon closer inspection, you realize that there is no right or wrong answer.

In some cases, it makes sense to recover for the same amount of time as your hard effort was. So if you run a hard 400m interval, a 400m recovery period is a viable option.

But if you're doing 2-mile hard intervals, you're probably not going to need an easy 2-mile jog to recover. Lord knows I wouldn't have the patience for that!

Perhaps the better option to determining how long your recovery interval needs to be is to listen to your body.

Recovering back to 100% isn't necessary, this is a workout after all! But once you feel like you're about 80% recovered, you're probably ready to start your next hard effort.

As with everything related to writing your training plan, determining the appropriate amount of time for your recovery period is a fair bit more art than science.

Do your best with trying to find the right balance, and don't hesitate to make some changes (if necessary) between one set and the next.

If it felt like your recovery period was too long, cut it down a bit. If it was too short, extend it.

And once you get it right, stick with it for the rest of the workout.

INTERVAL VARIATIONS

There are about a billion different variations of interval workouts that you can incorporate into your training plan.

Ok, maybe not a billion. But there are a lot of options, from which you can choose. And if you're creative, you can always come up with something new.

That said, here are some of the more common variations of interval workouts that you can add to your plan:

LONG INTERVALS

Mile repeats

These are pretty straightforward. A hard mile, followed by a recovery period. A suggested number of repeats: 2-6.

2-mile repeats

The same as above, with one minor difference: run two miles hard before your recovery period. A suggested number of repeats: 2-3.

Fartlek runs

A fartlek run, also referred to as speed play, is nothing but a loosey-goosey interval workout where the intervals aren't predetermined and aren't consistent. After you warm up, you randomly alternate between hard intervals and recovery periods for the duration of your workout. Hard intervals will likely range from a couple of hundred yards to a mile or more, and recovery times will vary accordingly. Just make sure you're dialing up the intensity regularly, and more importantly, have fun!

Timed intervals

With timed intervals, your focus isn't on covering a certain distance during your hard interval, but rather on maintaining a hard pace for a certain amount of time. A suggested number of repeats: 3-6, depending on duration.

SHORT INTERVALS

400m repeats

Pretty self-explanatory here. 400m hard, then catch your breath and do it all again. Suggested repeats: 6-12.

800m repeats

Same as the 400m repeats. Go hard for 800m (half of a mile) and then recover. Suggested repeats: 4-10.

Timed intervals

With timed intervals, your focus isn't on covering a certain distance during your hard interval, but rather on maintaining a hard pace for a certain amount of time. Suggested repeats: 10-20 depending on duration of interval and your fitness level.

Ladders/pyramids

A ladder or a pyramid workout incorporates different durations of hard intervals in the same workout. A sample ladder workout may start with a 30-second hard interval, followed by intervals of 60, 90, 120, and 150 seconds. Then, starting back at 30 and doing it all again. A pyramid workout will have a similar progression of the hard efforts, but instead of starting back at the beginning for round two, you'll work in reverse to the beginning. So a pyramid workout may look like 30, 60, 90, 120, 150, 120, 90, 60, 30.

HOW TO SCHEDULE YOUR WORKOUTS

Knowing the different types of workouts that your training plan should include is pretty straightforward.

Knowing how to incorporate them into your training? That is a bit trickier.

That said, there is a simple rule that I always follow both for myself and for my clients: hard workouts are *never* scheduled on back-to-back days.

Never.

Instead, I always make sure there is at least one, preferably two, days between hard workouts with either easy running days, cross training days, or rest days on the schedule. I also avoid putting a hard run either the day before or the day after a long run, in almost all cases.

By doing so, you are giving your body a chance to repair the cellular damage caused by one hard workout before you begin your next hard workout, which will help to minimize your risk of injury.

If you're still new to running or haven't done many hard workouts in the past, one hard day per week is plenty.

If you've been training consistently for many months/years and have a very solid base of fitness, you can probably get away with two hard training days per week.

That said, whether you're doing one day of hard training per week or two, always listen to your body and adjust accordingly. If you are sore and feeling fatigued, scrap the hard run altogether and just get some easy miles (or no miles at all) for that day.

THE TAPER

For many runners, the taper is one of the hardest parts of the training cycle.

The last two to three weeks of the training cycle are commonly referred to as the taper period, which is when you strategically dial back the volume of your training to allow the muscles in your legs to fully recover, so you'll be ready to run hard on the day of your race.

If you're preparing for your first race, that may sound easy enough. But let me assure you, abiding by the rules of the taper can be difficult.

Up to this point, you've been steadily progressing in your training to the point where you've run close to, or longer than, the distance of the race for which you are training.

And now, just a couple of weeks before the big day, you're supposed to cut back the amount of running substantially?

Yes, that's exactly what you're supposed to do.

Many runners assume, incorrectly, that by not running as much for the two weeks before the race, one of two things will happen:

Either they will lose some of the cardiovascular fitness, or they will be less than 100% ready for their race because they stopped training as intensely.

While I understand the logic of both scenarios, I promise you that neither fear is warranted.

In the first case, you won't lose much fitness in two weeks of decreased volume.

Yes, anyone who has ever taken a chunk of time off realizes that you can lose fitness quickly if you're not doing any running.

But guess what? You will still be running during your taper.

And as long as you're still doing some running, your body will hold on to the gains that you've made over the training cycle to this point.

I promise.

And even if you lose 0.001% of the fitness that you've built, you'll more than make up the difference by being fully rested and ready to go on the day of the race.

Now, if your fear is that you could still improve your fitness by continuing to train during your taper, please hear me out.

The kinds of physiological changes that would be beneficial on race day take a few weeks to show up in your body. So biologically speaking, any training that you're doing less than two weeks from the day of your race won't benefit you on race day.

However, if you keep increasing your training instead of abiding by the rules of the taper, your odds of being rested and refreshed for the race are next to zero.

So while it might sound good in your head to continue training at a high volume/intensity leading up to your race, don't do it!

Point blank, you'll be sabotaging your race if you don't abide by the rules of the taper.

And what are the rules of the taper?

I'm glad you asked.

RULES OF THE TAPER

The most important rule to follow during the taper period is to dial back on the volume of your training.

Cut back your long run to maybe 50% of your longest training run during the weeks of the taper. So for example, if three weeks before a half marathon you did 11 miles, two weeks before the half you might run eight miles and the week before you might run five or six.

This reduction in volume allows you to get a quality workout both weeks, but prevents excess wear and tear on your body and fatigue to your muscles.

You should also cut back on the volume of some of your other runs as well. Shortening the number of miles spent at tempo pace and decreasing the number of intervals during hard workouts would also be a good choice.

And depending on how you're feeling, it may be wise to omit a short run or two altogether.

Regarding intensity, the rules of the taper are a little more vague.

If you're feeling strong, it's ok to maintain the intensity of your training runs (tempo and/or intervals) more than a week before your race.

But the week of your race, you should probably keep everything short and easy. Just do a couple of runs, enough to break a sweat and burn off some nervous energy, and that's about it.

Also during the taper, you want to make sure that you are doing the other "little things" that are key to your success as a runner.

Make sure you're getting plenty of sleep. In fact, try to get a little extra sleep. Do some yoga. Spend some extra time on the foam roller. Eat plenty of fruits and veggies and be drinking more water than usual.

Do everything that you can do to tilt the odds in your favor so that you will be fully rested, recovered, and ready to go when the race starts.

But wait, there's more!

Another thing to be aware of during your taper period are the infamous taper pains. I've had bouts of taper pains several times, and I know many runners who have had similar experiences.

In a nutshell, a taper pain is something that randomly starts hurting for absolutely no reason.

It could be a knee. It could be a calf. It could be your foot.

It could be anything.

But when you're tapering, if something starts to hurt, don't freak out. I don't know what causes these pains, but random taper pains are all in your head.

Once the race starts and you're a mile or two in, the pains will disappear.

I promise.

SUMMARY

There is no universally "right" way of preparing for a race.

Every runner is different. Every race is different. And every training plan is different.

You have plenty of room to play with the various types of workouts that you may include in your training cycle, but please keep in mind that variety in your training is a good thing.

Remember, however, that the skeleton of a quality training plan is always going to be pretty much the same.

Maintain and improve your base

Your base level of fitness is super important, period.

If you don't have a solid base upon which to build, your training plan will crumble.

That said, your base level of fitness isn't something you can focus on once and then forget about. You always need to be monitoring your base, working to repair the little cracks and fissures that emerge during hard workouts, and adding to it whenever possible.

If you are serious about having a great race, you will take extra good care of your base.

It's that simple.

The different types of workouts you should be doing

To get the most out of your training and be ready to go hard on the day of your race, you need to incorporate a variety of different types of workouts into your training plan.

Each type of workout has its physiological benefits, and that is why you need to make sure to include each of the different types of training runs into your training plan.

A "balanced training diet" will give you your best chance of successfully nailing your goals on race day.

How to schedule your workouts intelligently

How you schedule the different workouts in your training plan is every bit as important as making sure that you have the different types of workouts in your plan from the beginning.

That said, there isn't a secret formula for how to schedule your workouts. Like many aspects of this process, it's a heavy pour of art mixed with a healthy dose of science.

A good suggestion is to make sure that you never do high-intensity workouts on back to back days. Always give yourself a day between tempo/speed sessions that is either a rest day, an easy day, or a cross-training day.

Respect the taper

Repeat after me: I will respect the taper.

Say it again. And again.

The taper can be the toughest part of training for many runners because it seems so counterintuitive that dialling back your training for 2+ weeks is going to help you more than it will hurt you.

But it will.

Dial back the mileage. Dial back the duration of your hard workouts.

Respect the taper and keep it holy. The payoff will be evident on race day.

To a non-runner, when you're preparing for a marathon or half marathon you simply need to run.

A lot.

But clearly, there is a lot more to becoming race ready than only "running."

It's ok to mix up the types of hard workouts you're regularly doing. In fact, I'd recommend it. But make sure that you're not too focused on the hard workouts. Those easy/recovery miles are essential to improving and solidifying your base, and they should not be overlooked.

And when it's all said and done, remember that the creation of your training plan is a mixture of art and science.

So if something doesn't seem to be working regarding how you schedule your workouts, keep tweaking your plan until it's right for you.

PRE-HAB

No runner wants to get injured while training for a race.

Yet, it happens. Often.

While it's impossible to prevent every potential running-related injury, something that gets overlooked by many of us non-elite runners is the importance of proactively working to prevent an injury in the first place.

Instead, we worry about our workouts and wonder if we are doing enough, and then when something starts to hurt we try to duct tape it together until after the race.

I'm sure you don't do that, right?

Riiiiiiiight...

If you'd rather avoid an injury instead of being forced to deal with it, you need to embrace preventative exercises, aka pre-hab.

In this chapter, we will be going over three of the most important, and often overlooked, aspects of a good pre-hab routine:

- Strength training.
- Recovery.
- Flexibility.

Please keep in mind that none of these activities, in isolation, are a magic bullet to injury prevention.

But, if you are consistently incorporating each pre-hab activity into your routine, you will significantly reduce your risk of developing a running-related injury in the build-up to your race.

STRENGTH TRAINING

Strength training is one of the most important, yet neglected, components of the average runner's routine. And if it's not part of your routine, odds of you including it in your training for your race are even lower.

But if you want to be ready on race day, you're going to need to make regular strength training a priority.

Now to be clear, I'm not suggesting for one moment that you need to spend an hour or more at the gym 4-5 times per week in addition to your running.

Seriously, ain't nobody got time for that!

What I am suggesting is that you spend at least 15-20 minutes a couple of days each week doing some strength training exercises to help improve your running performance and decrease your chance of injury.

That's it.

And if your life is so crazy that you can't come up with 15-20 minutes after a run, you can add your strength training in at other times of the week as you're able. However, immediately after a run, and specifically a hard run/workout, is ideal.

Why? Because after a hard workout the muscles in your legs are already fatigued from the workout you just did. So this is prime time to get the biggest bang for your buck when it comes to your strength training.

One thing that you want to avoid, in most cases, is doing your strength training on rest days.

We will talk about rest days much more in another page or two, but please don't sacrifice a rest day by making it a strength training day. Just don't.

COMMON EXCUSES

Whenever I talk about strength training with runners, the two objections to strength training that I hear most often are not having enough time and not having a gym membership/equipment at home.

Neither is a good excuse.

Again, you don't need a lot of time. Seriously, 15-20 minutes is more than enough time to meet your strength training needs in most cases.

And if finding 15-20 minutes for some much-needed strength training is that difficult, you can multitask so you're getting your strength training in while you're doing other things at the same time.

- Do lunges and/or squats while dinner (or breakfast) is cooking on the stove.

- Do wall sits or toe raises while you are brushing your teeth.
- Do pushups and planks while you're on the floor playing with your kids or fooling around on social media.

Honestly, the ways that you can "invent time" for strength training through your day are almost limitless. Get creative and make it happen.

And when it comes to feeling like you need to have a gym membership or a bunch of equipment at your house, that's just crazy!

Sure, having some different tools allows for a larger variety of exercises that you can do, but by using nothing but your body weight, you can easily work the muscles that will benefit you as a runner.

Not sure where to start when it comes to strength training? Head to the resources page at the back of the book, and I've got you covered!

Another excuse to avoid strength training that I hear on occasion is the fear that strength training is going to cause you to build too much muscle mass and negatively impact your running.

Stop. Just stop.

It's not going to happen, and here's why:

To build serious muscle mass, you need to lift serious amounts of weight over, and over, and over again.

Simply put, that's not what you'll be doing.

Even if you own your equipment and/or have a gym membership so that you're able to lift heavy on occasion, you aren't going to pack on the type of mass that could impact your running by accident.

I promise.

And ladies, you definitely don't have to worry about adding too much mass because you're short on the most important factor when it comes to building muscle size: testosterone.

Seriously, you need to make regular strength training a regular part of your routine.

It's that important.

RECOVERY

Newsflash, running is hard on the body!

Pounding out the miles, even easy/recovery miles, day after day and month after month (and year after year) takes a toll on your body.

Fortunately, our bodies are magnificent at taking care of themselves and adapting to the demands we place upon them.

Unless, of course, we don't give our bodies a chance to recover.

Recovery time is of vital importance, and we get it one of two ways: days off and while sleeping.

DAYS OFF

Regular rest days are every bit as important to your overall training plan as any of the running workouts that you are going to do during your training cycle.

No joke.

I tell my clients that they should treat their rest days the same way they treat any other day of their training plan. You run on the days your plan says to run, and you don't run on the days your plan tells you to rest.

It's that simple.

SLEEP

While a rest day is important to give your body (and mind) a break during a training cycle, there is no substitute for a good night's sleep. When you are sleeping, your body is doing the necessary repair work at the cellular level to prevent you from breaking down.

While we rest, our cells are repairing the damage that we cause during our workouts, as well as from our daily activities.

And this is the process that enables us to get stronger and faster.

When you don't get enough sleep, you are sabotaging the training that you are doing.

That is how important sleep is to your success as a runner.

So if staying healthy and reaching your goals on race day are important to you, make sure you're getting enough sleep throughout the entire training cycle.

FLEXIBILITY

Runners are a notoriously inflexible bunch.

And while there is no scientifically backed proof that stretching prevents injuries from occurring, there is no question that a reduced range of motion can be a contributing factor for many running related injuries.

Improving, or at the very least maintaining, your flexibility is a good thing.

How do you do it?

STRETCHING

Static stretching after a run is a good thing.

A post-run stretch helps to relieve tension in the muscles and improve blood flow to the tissue, which is going to speed recovery and reduce soreness.

OTHER SUGGESTIONS

Improving your strength, getting enough rest, and becoming more flexible are all beneficial when it comes to reducing your risk of injury during your training cycle.

But here are a few other tricks of the trade that I'd definitely encourage you to make a regular part of your pre-hab routine if they aren't already:

FOAM ROLLING

If you don't have a foam roller, put the book down right now and order one.

Now.

A foam roller is one of the most important pre-hab items in the toolbox of any runner.

You can use your foam roller to give yourself a massage. You can use your foam roller to loosen tight muscles.

You can use your foam roller to torment your dog and you can use it in place of a toy for your toddler. (Not that I know from experience or anything...)

Point being, your foam roller is versatile for minimizing/getting rid of the aches and pains that you will encounter during your training cycle.

And the best part of all, it's practically idiot-proof to use!

- Lay the foam roller on the ground.
- Put the body part you want to work on top of the roller.
- Roll back and forth.

That's it.

You can roll an entire muscle group, or you can focus on one spot and just rock back and forth on the most tender area while you fight back the tears.

I would encourage you to make a regular practice of rolling your calves, hamstrings, and IT bands. I'm also a fan of rolling my quads, glutes, and hip flexors, but I may be a bit of a glutton for punishment.

GOLF BALL

Want to know my secret weapon for combating plantar fasciitis?

Titleist.

Or Top Flite. Or Nike. Or Slazenger.

The type of golf ball makes absolutely no difference, but I haven't found anything that loosens up a tight plantar fascia like a golf ball.

I keep a golf ball at my desk, and when I think of it, I simply put it on the floor and massage my foot while I'm working.

Roll your foot back and forth from the ball of your feet to your heel a couple of times per week, and that's often enough to eliminate plantar fasciitis from the equation.

And if you want to up the ante, keep a golf ball in your freezer.

The combination of cold and massage is fantastic.

YOGA

Yoga is a beautiful thing.

Not only is yoga good for helping to improve your flexibility, but depending on the type of yoga you are doing it can also be great for building strength and stability in both your core and your legs.

There are a lot of options for including regular yoga into your routine as you prepare for your race.

You can take classes from a yoga studio, and if you're a member at a gym, you may want to check what, if any, yoga classes are available with your membership.

But you can also dial up YouTube for some great free yoga routines that you can do from the comfort of your living room.

Not sure where to start? Try Yoga with Adrien.

She has a couple of hundred free videos on YouTube, ranging in length from 10 minutes to over an hour. She even has one or two that are specifically for runners, so feel free to start there.

SUMMARY

Benjamin Franklin once said that an ounce of prevention is worth a pound of cure.

And in this case, he was correct.

The last thing you want to deal with during your training cycle is an injury.

So do yourself a favor by being proactive when it comes to preventing running injuries.

It's time well spent, I promise.

Strength training

Don't be the kind of runner that thinks that strength training won't help you.

Please.

There are enough benefits of strength training for runners that entire books have been written on the subject.

Why is strength training for runners so necessary? Not only will it help reduce your risk of sustaining a running-related injury, but it will also help you perform better on race day.

You don't need a gym membership, and you don't need to devote lots of time to your strength training to get the benefits of strength training either.

Devoting 15-20 minutes two or three times per week in your living room is plenty, I promise.

Not sure where/how to proceed? Check out the resources page at the back of the book for some strength training exercise suggestions to help you get started.

Recovery

Point blank, if you don't allow your body enough time to recover it will eventually break down.

And while there is something to be said for easy/recovery runs as part of your training plan, getting enough sleep and having scheduled days off are vital to allowing your body a chance to repair the damage caused by training.

Please, don't undermine yourself by failing to allow enough time for recovery throughout the entirety of your training cycle.

Flexibility

Very few runners would be considered overly flexible, so working on improving/maintaining your flexibility is a good idea.

Having muscles that are incredibly tight can definitely lead to a variety of overuse injuries, especially in repetitive motion sports like running. Also, tight muscles reduce your range of motion, which forces your body to do more work to get from the start line to the finish line.

Keep that in mind the next time you don't think you have time to stretch after a run.

There are a couple of other activities that I do on a regular basis to help improve my flexibility and reduce the risk that I'll wind up injured because of my running.

Yoga, foam rolling, and golf ball massage are all regular parts of my daily/weekly flexibility program.

And I would definitely encourage you to make them a regular part of yours as well.

One thing that I want to make clear is that completely eliminating the chance of sustaining a running-related injury is impossible.

That said, remember that an ounce of prevention is almost always worth a pound of cure.

Yes, pre-hab requires a little extra time and effort.

Yes, you have to *do* the pre-hab for it to be effective.

But it's a small price to pay to give you the best chance of getting to race day healthy, fully trained, and ready to go.

ADJUST ON THE FLY

"Everybody has a plan until they get punched in the face."

~Mike Tyson

I'm a sucker for a good quote, and that Tyson quote is a gem if ever there was one.

Hopefully, you don't have to worry about literally getting punched in the face while you're preparing for your race, but there will almost certainly be a point during your training cycle that life will metaphorically punch you in the mouth and you will have to adjust.

While you are training for your race, life is going to happen.

How you respond to life will go a long way in determining how you do on race day.

In this chapter, I will help you know how to respond no matter how many jabs, crosses, hooks, or uppercuts you face while preparing for your race.

These are some of the most common metaphorical punches you'll need to watch out for when you're preparing for your race:

- How to handle the days that you can't run.
- Remember, no one run is "do or die."
- How to shift workouts around.
- Managing the aches and pains.

Training for a race is hard enough without having to bob and weave your way through the next few months trying to avoid a life-size haymaker.

Don't worry.

This chapter will serve as the corner man you need to help you make the adjustments necessary to stay on track with your training and be ready on race day.

As for all of the boxing references? You're welcome.

Time to answer the bell!

HOW TO HANDLE THE DAYS THAT YOU CAN'T RUN

Odds are, you're not going to do every single run that is in your training plan.

Something is going to happen over the 16ish weeks that you are training for your race that is going to cause you to miss a run.

You might oversleep. Your kids could get sick. You may have to work late.

The list of perfectly valid reasons for missing a run could go on and on, but the point is that doing every run on your training plan is more likely the exception than the rule.

So if the odds are that you're going to miss at least one run during your training cycle, the question becomes how do you react when that happens?

Simple.

Let it go.

REMEMBER, NO ONE RUN IS "DO OR DIE"

I know, telling you to forget about a missed run is much easier for me to say than for you to do, right?

Right.

But the fact of the matter is that there is no such thing as a run that is "do or die" when it comes to being prepared for a race.

Sure, some runs are a bit more valuable than others, but missing any single run has virtually zero impact on your overall fitness on race day.

Keep that in mind when you catch a right hook to the chin courtesy of life.

HOW TO SHIFT WORKOUTS AROUND

When life staggers you, and you find yourself in a neutral corner for a standing eight count (seriously, how much longer can I keep dishing up boxing metaphors?), you may need to adjust your training plan to help you get back on track.

How?

Well, it depends.

How many workouts did you miss? What kinds of workouts were they (easy runs, long runs, tempo, intervals)? Where are you in your training plan? How many other workouts have you missed in this training cycle?

There are dozens of questions that will help to determine how you should adjust your training plan to help you get back up to speed. And as such, it is important to remember that there is no one right way to do so.

As with the initial creation of your training plan, adapting/adjusting your plan due to life is more art than science.

That said, here are a few guidelines that may help you determine what you should do when it comes to adapting/adjusting to a missed training run:

- Don't try to make up for missing an easy run. Seriously, let those few easy miles go completely and don't look back for a second.

- If you miss a long run, don't try to do more next week to "make up" for the one you missed. Instead, split the difference between the workout you missed and the workout that is next on your schedule and do that distance for your next long run. So if you missed a ten miler, and your next scheduled run is for 12 miles, simply do 11 instead. Then the following week, do whatever is scheduled and keep right on trucking.

- Missed interval/tempo workouts can be tricky when it comes to trying to adapt your plan. Remember, you never want to do hard workouts on back-to-back days. So based on your schedule, you may be limited in your ability to make up for your missed run. The best advice, then, is to let it go if at all possible. If you're the kind of person that struggles with missing a hard workout, remember that if you're going to try and make it up (which is not what I would recommend just so we are clear on that point), you don't want to have hard workouts on back-to-back days. So if your hard days are Tuesday and Thursday, like mine typically are, a missed Tuesday workout really can't be made up without messing up the rest of the week's plan.

If I were going to try and give you an IFTTT formula for every possible scenario that you could face when it comes to adapting and adjusting to life during your training plan, this book would get rather long.

Like Gone With the Wind long.

Instead, let me just remind you that adapting and adjusting your training plan is more art than science. So make a decision and go with it.

And remember, no training run is do or die.

DEALING WITH ACHES AND PAINS

Running is a contact sport.

Clearly, it's not on the same level as football, rugby, or ice hockey, but consider how many times your foot hits the ground over the course of every run. Then think about the amount of force that your body is absorbing with each foot strike.

So yeah, running is a contact sport.

And as with any other contact sport, injuries can and do happen.

When an injury or a concerning ache/pain pops up, you'll need to adjust your training accordingly. Failing to do so is asking for your situation to only become worse, so the quicker you can address the issue and adapt your training plan, the better!

How do you adapt your plan?

That is the million dollar question, and I wish I could give you a million dollar answer.

Sadly, I can't.

There is no one-size-fits-all type of answer to give here because there are *way* too many variables at play. Where you feel the pain, when you experience it, and how severe it is are just a few of the questions I would need to know the answers to before I could offer substantive advice for amending your training based on the aches and pains you are experiencing.

That said, a safe piece of advice is to get it checked out asap. Whether that's seeing your doctor, a physical therapist, a chiropractor, or some other medical professional, it's wise to get an expert's opinion on your issue to avoid doing something foolish (like continuing to run) that is only going to make the problem worse.

Another nearly universal piece of advice would be to stop running, at least for a few days, and try to get a little extra rest. Allowing your body to do what it does best—repair itself—may be all you need to do to avoid missing any serious time from your training due to a particular ache/pain or minor injury.

You may also want to consider doing some non-impact cardio to help maintain your fitness. Jump on the bike, dive in the pool, get on the rowing machine—whatever it is, just keep doing something to stay active as long as it doesn't irritate whatever it is that's bothering you.

Unless, of course, you see a doctor/therapist who tells you to rest. In that case, and as difficult as that may be for you, the best thing you can do is nothing.

SUMMARY

While you are training for your race, life is going to punch you in the face.

Period. End of. Full stop.

When that happens, you have two choices: counterpunch or throw in the towel.

And let's be real, there is no way you're going to throw in the towel.

I guess you only have one choice then, eh?

In that case, here are a few things to keep in mind while you are counterpunching.

Days you can't run

There will be days that you're scheduled to run that you simply can't make the run happen.

Whether you're sick, you have to work late, you have to take care of the kids, or any number of other issues that can crop up at the last minute, please remember that if you can't run for a day, it will be ok.

No one run is "do or die"

And this is why it will be ok when you are forced to miss a run. Nothing on your training plan is do or die when it comes to making sure you are ready to go on race day.

Are some runs more valuable than others over the course of preparing for your race?

Yeah, probably. But if you are forced to miss a workout it will not derail you from being ready for your race.

Shifting workouts around

When life lands a couple of punches, and your plan starts to fall apart, stay calm and look for a way to counter.

And in many cases, that means shifting your workouts.

This is why I advised you to avoid writing more than a week or two of workouts at a time because odds are you're going to have to move things around a few times over the course of your training cycle.

If you need to change things up a bit, that's fine. If you need to bump one type of workout for another, that's fine.

Just make sure you don't do hard workouts on back-to-back days, and preferably neither the day before or after a long run.

Other than that, shuffle your schedule to your heart's content.

Aches and pains

Running, like boxing, is a contact sport.

As such, you are likely to experience some bumps, bruises, and possibly a little bit of bloodshed along the way.

That said, always remember to listen to your body. If something is hurting while you are running, it would probably be a good idea to give yourself a few extra days of rest and get your issue checked out.

For the most part, ignoring an issue isn't going to make it better. In fact, it's probably going to make it worse.

Don't try to power through an ache or a pain foolishly, because odds are it'll end up costing you more than it would have if you just addressed it when you first noticed the symptoms.

Having a training plan is a good thing, but how you adapt your plan based on the punches life throws your way is the key to having a solid (and successful) training cycle.

Do your best to keep your hands up to protect yourself from the punches that will be coming your way, but when one connects, you now have the ammunition you need to brush it off and keep pressing forward.

You got this, champ!

FINAL PREPARATIONS

One mistake that I see many runners make, and that I may also be guilty of making on occasion, is showing up to the start of a race unprepared.

Logging your miles in the months leading up to a race is clearly an important part of the preparation for your race.

But that's only part of the process. And if you only do part of the process, no matter how well you do that part, you're still going to be unprepared.

To be fully prepared and ready to go on race day, make sure you do the following things a week to 10 days before the big day:

- Honestly assess your training.
- Reassess your goals.
- Double check the course profile.
- Develop a specific strategy for the race.

Why is this important? There will likely be a lot of changes between the start of your training cycle and the race.

Taking the time to plan for your race ensures that the race you run is the race for which you trained.

HONESTLY ASSESS YOUR TRAINING

How did your training go?

Honestly.

Have you been feeling strong and been able to get in almost all of your runs? Has life been its unpredictable, and you've been struggling to simply keep your head above water?

On the whole, how would you assess what you've done during this training cycle?

Looking back at your entire training cycle as race day approaches is an important step that is easy to overlook.

Why is it so important?

Because at this point, it's too late to make any significant changes to your level of fitness. The race is going to happen in a few days, and for lack of a better way to say it you are now officially as physically ready as you're going to be.

And everything else that you should be doing to make your final preparations for the race hinge on you having done an honest assessment of your training first.

REASSESSING GOALS

Once you've assessed how your training went, it's time to look back at your goals for the race and redefine them accordingly.

Based on an honest look at your training, you will need to decide if you should have a more aggressive goal, a less aggressive one, or stand pat with the goal that was set when you started the training cycle.

There is absolutely nothing wrong with adjusting your target a few days before a race. In fact, I'd argue that it might be wiser to wait until just a few days before your race to set your specific goals than to try to put goals in place at the beginning of a 16+ week training cycle.

Now that your goal is re-established, what's next?

DOUBLE CHECK COURSE SPECIFICS

Not all halfs/fulls are created equal.

Every race is unique, and as such, every race has its little nuances that need to be taken into account before you decide how you want to run the race.

Is the race pancake flat? Are there rolling hills? Lots of twists and turns? Basically a straight shot?

Take the time to check out the race's website in the days leading up to the race to remind yourself what you're getting into beyond the 13.1 or 26.2 miles.

STRATEGY FOR RACE DAY

Now for the fun stuff.

At this point, you're going to put it all together and formulate what you want to do once the race starts.

Based on an honest assessment of your training cycle and a fresh look at the course specifics, you've dialed in your goal for this race.

Now you need a plan for how to get there.

Why? A plan is important because research shows that you are 20% more likely to reach your goal if you follow a plan.

And I'm sorry to break it to you, but a good plan for hitting your goal is much more in-depth than simply picking a time goal and using a pace calculator to determine what your average pace needs to be to cross the finish line under your goal.

That said, knowing what your average pace needs to be is certainly a valuable piece of information that you should use while coming up with your strategy for race day.

RACE PACE STRATEGY

Pacing yourself over the course of an entire half or full marathon is tough. (Dare I say it's more art than science, or have I used that analogy to death already?)

Point blank, it's easy to look at a pace calculator and determine that if your goal is to finish in X, you need to run each mile in Y.

But like many things in life, it's rarely that simple.

The generally accepted goal in endurance racing is the negative split, meaning that you finish the second half of your race slightly faster than the first half. To do that, you can't just try to run the same exact pace from the start of the race to the finish. Instead, you'll want to start off slightly slower than your goal pace, settle into your pace after a few miles, and then have enough left in the tank to pick up the pace slightly over the last couple of miles.

Easy enough right?

Rrrrriiiiiiiigggggggghhhhhhhhttttttt....

On paper, negative splits are a piece of cake. In actuality, they are quite a bit more difficult.

Managing your pace at the start of a race can be a struggle for many runners for two big reasons: adrenaline and fresh legs.

The start of a race, especially one with thousands of runners participating, is often a festive environment. Between music blasting, the final countdown to the beginning of the race, and the possibility of fireworks when the gun goes off, it's easy for even the most experienced runners to get more than a little amped up at the start of a race.

Add to that being in a sea of runners that are all equally excited, and it's easy to end up running the first couple of miles closer to tempo pace than the goal race pace.

True story, when I ran my first marathon (and was dreadfully ill-prepared) my goal for the race was to average 10-minute miles. I started out a little fast but figured I'd be ok after the first mile or so. However, after the first mile, the course narrowed, and we ran through a tunnel of spectators that were all yelling and screaming and cheering for us for about a quarter of a mile.

I vividly remember feeling like I was floating during that quarter mile stretch and chatting for a moment with the guy next to me. I randomly checked my watch and saw that my current pace was 7:34.

Uh-oh.

In hindsight, it's clear to me that I was so caught up in the excitement of the start of my first marathon (and first race longer than 10k) that I simply couldn't control my pace.

In addition to the extra adrenaline you're likely to experience at the start of a race, having fresh legs can also lead to a start that is too fast.

A properly executed taper period is necessary to make sure you're rested and ready to go at the start of the race. We've already established that. But after your taper period, there is a good chance your legs will feel better than they have felt in months.

And because of this, it's easy to go out too quickly.

Between the adrenaline rush and your fresh legs, running a minute or two per mile faster than your targeted goal pace is likely to feel comfortable.

Perhaps almost too comfortable. For a few miles.

Problem: your race is longer than a few miles.

Properly managing the first few miles of your race won't guarantee that you nail your race goal. But if you go out too fast, you can pretty much count on having a rough second half to your race.

RUNNING A SMART RACE

In addition to managing the start of your race in order to avoid starting too fast and blowing up well before the finish line, there are a number of other things you would be wise to remember on race day.

RUN THE TANGENTS

The shortest distance between two points is a straight line, yes?

Sorry for the flashback to your high school geometry class, but this is important.

Odds are, the route you're running for your race isn't going to be a straight line.

And that is why running the tangents are beneficial. The tangents are the shortest route around the turns of the roads/paths of the course.

And a certified course is measured along the tangents.

If you fail to run the tangents, your actual race distance will be longer than the 13.1 or 26.2 miles you signed up to run.

So what are the tangents for a race? Simply put, the tangents are the inside of any corner or turn.

Turning to the right? Get as far to the right as you can. Going left? Be left.

Pretty simple, eh?

And in case you're wondering how much of a difference running the tangents makes, it can be huge.

In my second marathon, when I got to the finish line my Garmin read 26.68 miles. By not being focused on running the tangent lines of the course, I'd added almost a half of a mile to my race.

And at the end of a marathon, a half of a mile is a lot! And when it comes to your PRs or BQs, you can't just stop your watch and call it a day when your watch shows you're at 13.1 or 26.2 miles.

You've got to get to the finish line for your time to officially count, so you might as well do so as efficiently as possible.

Run the tangents, as much as you can, to avoid adding any extra distance to your race.

PLAN FOR THE HILLS

Very few races are legitimately pancake flat.

Sure, there are lots of races that advertise themselves as "flat and fast," but most of those races have some incline/decline that you're going to have to navigate during your race.

So be prepared.

And I don't mean be prepared in the sense of making sure you run some hill repeats and maybe include a couple of hills in most of your training runs. I mean be prepared in the sense of knowing when they are coming and what you are going to do when you get to them.

Believe me; there is a difference between a hill at Mile 2 and the same hill at Mile 20.

If the hills are early in the race, you know you're going to need to stay composed and avoid using up too much energy while you're going up them. But if they are late in the race, you may have an easier time "allowing" yourself to walk up the hills to save a bit of energy for a finish line kick.

And if you know that the finish is right on top of a little hill at the end of the race, you know you can sell out completely when you get to the final hill.

When I talked with Sage Canaday in the early days of the podcast (dizruns.com/020), he said something that has stuck with me ever since. He said there is no reason to run up a hill when you can walk up that same hill just as fast.

Think about that for a minute.

If you're in the early stages of a race, or any stage really, and the hill is long and steep, the best strategy may be to not run up the hill.

And in case you're unaware, Sage is no slouch. He's legitimately one of the top trail/mountain/ultra runners/racers in the world. So if one of the best runners in the world can force himself not to try to run up every big hill that he sees during a race, maybe we need to be humble enough to be ok with walking ourselves.

FUEL/HYDRATION STRATEGY

Another aspect of your race day strategy that you need to account for, and that is easy to overlook, is your fueling/hydration strategy.

When I was new to running and racing, I used to never worry about how I'd fuel at a race. Races had water/sports drinks available, and most events handed out food at a few places along the course as well.

Yeah, that may not be the best course of action.

Yes, most races will have some provisions available during the race. And there's nothing wrong with using what's available as necessary.

But unless you've been training using the exact fuel sources/brand of drink that will be available, you will be running the risk of having some GI issues from ingesting something different than usual on race day. This is especially true if you have a sensitive stomach.

A proper fuel/hydration strategy is much more than just worrying about what you'll take in during your race, however. You also need to think about the foods you're consuming a day or two before your race and what (if anything) you're eating in the morning before your race.

And when is the best time to figure all of this stuff out?

During your training, and specifically during your long runs.

Keep notes of what you're taking in the night before, the morning of, and during your long runs and how you feel during your training runs.

If you keep notes and aren't afraid to experiment, you'll start to see a pattern emerge as to what you need to do to run your best on race day.

Me? I can pretty much eat whatever the night before, as long as I'm staying away from things that are overly greasy. On the morning of the race, I need to eat.

Not just a bagel or a piece of fruit either; *I need food!* All the eggs! All the potatoes! A piece or two of toast! Coffee by the pot!

And then during the race, some fruit (especially an orange) is the perfect fuel source for me. Mix in some sports drink, the stronger the better, and some water and I'm ready to go.

I found all of this out through trial and error while training for a race. The mornings I ate a big breakfast, and specifically one that *did not* include bacon or sausage, I felt like I could run forever.

You need to do the same thing. Try running after a big breakfast. Try running without any breakfast. Try running with a small bite and a consistent source of calories throughout.

The moral of the story with your fueling strategy is that you need to experiment during your training so that when race day comes, you can dial in on exactly what you need to do, and then you need to do it.

SUMMARY

As the race approaches, it's a good idea to take the time to make sure that you're ready to go mentally as well as physically.

Feelings of nervousness before are perfectly normal. And in some cases, that little bit of nervous energy can be beneficial.

But too much nervous energy can quickly turn from a positive to a negative.

The suggestions in this chapter will help you keep your mind in the right place as race day approaches, and allow you to be ready to go when the gun goes off and the race begins.

If you take care of the things that we talked about in this chapter, you'll be confident in knowing that you're ready to go at the start of your race, nerves be damned.

As a reminder, make sure to:

Look back at the quality of your training cycle

Now that the heavy lifting of your training has wrapped up, how did it go?

Were you able to stick to the script pretty closely, or did life cause you to miss a few too many of your scheduled runs?

Now is the time to be 100% honest with yourself about how your training has gone. Look back at your data on Strava or RunKeeper or wherever you sync your watch and analyze the quality of your workouts.

Were they better than expected? Not so good? Somewhere in the middle?

Taking the time to look back will help you to move forward to the race.

Reassess your goals

Are the goals you set at the beginning of your training cycle still the right goals for you for this race?

That depends on how the training cycle went.

Based on your honest reflection on the past few months of training, it's time to decide whether your original goal is still the target or if you need to reassess things before the race.

If your training cycle was fantastic, maybe you should think about setting your sights a little bit higher.

If training went according to plan, stick to the original goal.

But if your training took an unexpected detour along the way, it may be wise to walk back your expectations slightly.

Clearly, backtracking on your goals isn't the ideal scenario.

But sometimes life happens. And when it does, you may have to adapt your plan to the current situation.

Hate to say it, but that's another glorious example of running imitating life.

Re-check the course profile

Double checking the layout of the course you will be racing is important to ensure that there are no surprises on race day.

When you looked at the profile of the course you are running in the early stages of writing your plan, you were looking for the general layout of the course. You were seeking to get an idea if the course was mostly flat or if there were hills you needed to train for during the race.

But now, you want to look for specifics.

Remind yourself exactly where the climbs are. Know where you'll get the benefit of a long gradual downhill or a pretty flat section.

Pay attention to where the long, straight sections of the course are located, or if there are any u-turns that you're going to have to navigate.

Know where these areas of the course are so that you won't be surprised by some giant hill with only a mile or two to go. If you know it's there, you can make sure to save some energy to power up that last climb (and pass a lot of people in the process).

Strategy for race day

The final thing you need to do before race day is to dial in the strategy you will follow for the race.

Are you going to try and negative split the race? Run it even? Go for broke with the understanding that a crash and a burn may be in your future?

Whatever your strategy, have it nailed down before you get to the race, ok?

Opting to try and "figure it out" as you go is most likely going to end poorly for you. There's no guarantee that having a solid strategy in place is going to result in you hitting your goals every time, but it will certainly help.

If you're not sure you need to take the time to plan your race out before you get to the starting line, I have one piece of advice for you: *make it happen.*

And let's not forget, in the week before your race you're not going to be running as much as usual, so you will have the time available.

At this point, you've done the physical work. Don't let that work be done in vain because you failed to prepare mentally for the race you're about to run.

POST-RACE RECOVERY

Despite what you may believe, your training plan doesn't end on race day.

What you do post-race is *almost* as important to your long-term success as a runner as what you do leading up to the race.

And in my experience, the best thing you can do is decide on your post-race recovery plans *before* the race. If you wait until after the race to plan the recovery phase, your results are likely to impact your decision-making process.

Make a plan before your race takes place, and then stick to it no matter how the race goes.

What should your recovery plan include?

- No running.
- Lots of movement.
- Ease back in.

These three little things may sound pretty straightforward, but sticking to them after a race can be a challenge. Believe me.

However, for your long-term health and sanity, adhering to these principals coming out of a training cycle is strongly recommended.

NO RUNNING

On the surface, this is pretty simple, eh? Don't run after the race, got it?

Good, but before we move on, we need to unpack this simple rule a little bit more.

No running after a race is pretty universally accepted, but for how long? For a few days? Until any soreness is gone? For a month or more?

One rule of thumb that I see tossed around from time to time is that you should take one day off for every mile that you're racing. So after a half marathon, you should avoid running for at least 13 days, and after a marathon, you should refrain from running for almost an entire month.

Sorry, but I have a hard time buying into that logic.

Yes, rest is important. And yes, most runners need to take more time off after a race than they think they do.

But to put a generic blanket statement out there for everyone to follow just doesn't make much sense to me.

One-size-fits-none, remember?

Instead of recommending a set amount of time to wait before running again after a race, I'm going to ask you to be honest with yourself about how you feel after your race has finished.

As long as you have some lingering achiness/soreness, the rec-ommendation is simple: don't run.

And that lingering achiness/soreness applies to everything that you're doing. Walking needs to be completely pain-free in all muscles and joints. Same thing for going up and down steps, getting out of a chair, or sitting down on the toilet. As long as you're experiencing any pain or discomfort in any part of your body post-race, you're to abstain from running.

So depending on the quality/quantity of your training, your level of fitness before the race, and the distance of your race, your time off from running could be a few days. It could also be a few weeks. Or more.

Once you are 100% pain-free, wait for three more days. Once you're pain-free plus three, then it's time to start getting back into your running routine.

More on that in a moment.

LOTS OF MOVEMENT

What, if anything, do you do between the end of the race and the time you start running again?

The simple answer: move. The slightly less simple answer: any movement, other than running, that's not overly intense. Walking. An easy bike ride. Yoga. Swimming.

Nothing crazy. Just enough to get your heart beating a little bit and maybe break a sweat.

As the achiness/discomfort starts to dissipate, you can up the intensity and duration of your non-running workouts.

Don't do too much too quickly, but getting your blood flowing will be good for you mentally and will help speed up the recovery process.

EASE BACK IN

After the post-race soreness has gone, you're probably going to be ready to get back out there and dive into running again.

And let's be honest, if you took as much time off as you should have after the race, you're probably going to be more than ready!

However, I need you to remember one thing: *take it easy!*

Once you start running again after allowing enough time to recover from your race you have one goal: solidify your base. Sound familiar?

No matter how solid your base was throughout your training cycle, racing hard is going to create a few cracks in your foundation that you need to address.

And that means that your return to running should be a handful of easy runs without any pizazz.

No speed work. No tempo runs. No long runs. Not yet.

Those workouts will come, I promise. But first things first, you need to focus on rebuilding your base.

After several easy runs, you can start to ramp things up over the course of a week or two until you're back to your normal training load. And don't forget that the higher the intensity of your workouts, the harder it is on your body.

So when you start to include some more intense workouts into your training again, don't just jump right into quarter mile repeats as hard as you can go! Instead, start with something around race pace (a couple of fartlek segments perhaps?) and work up to the higher intensity workouts over the next few weeks.

SUMMARY

If you only learn one thing from this chapter, please remember that your training plan doesn't end on race day!

It continues beyond the race until you're fully recovered.

Too many runners don't have a plan for what they should be doing after their race. As a result, they don't give their bodies or their minds the time needed to recover from the race and the odds of injury or burnout dramatically increase.

Please, don't make that mistake!

If you've been with me up to this point, stay with me just a little while longer.

Have a plan in place for after your race and stick to it!

No running

After a long training cycle and running a hard race, your body needs a break.

How long of a break? It depends on a lot of variables, so it's impossible to give a one-size-fits-all timeline.

That said, the vast majority of recreationally competitive runners that I know and talk to take dramatically less rest after a race than they should. So most likely, you need to take more time off than you think you do.

My simple rule is to wait until you feel 100% recovered from your race and are experiencing no residual soreness that could be attributed to the race, and then wait three more days to start running again.

That could be a few days for some runners and a few weeks for others.

Just do yourself a favor and err on the side of caution after a race. I promise nothing bad will happen if you take an extra few days of rest after your race.

Keep moving

Just because you're not running after your race doesn't mean you're sitting around doing nothing while you recover.

Our bodies were made to move, so move! Just don't run.

Go for long walks with the dogs. Go hiking. Splash in the pool with your kids. Jump on the bike for a tour of the neighborhood. Get out your mat and do some yoga.

What you do isn't as important as the act of simply doing with one caveat: *don't run!*

Another good idea is to avoid doing anything too intense.

So an easy swim in the pool or splashing with the kids is fine, but doing a hard pool workout is probably not the best idea.

Ease back in

Once you're ready to start running again, take your time and ease back into your regular running routine over the course of 10+ days.

Start with some easy runs that are relatively short to help shake the rust off and assess how you're feeling.

After a few of those, start upping the distance a bit while keeping the intensity low.

Finally, start bumping up the intensity a little bit at a time.

Point blank, consider the few weeks after your race as part of your training plan and take the time to map out what that recovery process will look like before your race.

Then stick to the plan.

You didn't willy-nilly your training, so don't willy-nilly your recovery either.

Deal?

CLOSING THOUGHTS

You made it.

You're ready.

At this point, you honestly know everything you need to know to create the training plan that *you* need to make sure that you are ready on race day.

The only thing that is missing at this point is the plan.

You have all the pieces to put it together, and you know every step I take when I'm creating a plan for my clients.

I promise you that nothing has been left out.

Now it's time to get started.

If your plan doesn't feel like it is 100% perfect from the get go, try to relax.

Creating a training plan is more art than science remember. And as such, no matter what you do it'll never be "perfect."

The beauty of my system is that you can make subtle changes week to week—shoot, you can make them day to day—so that the plan fits you and no one else.

You know enough. Now take action.

And do me a favor, eh?

Shoot me an email (diz@dizruns.com) with a photo of you and your bling after your race, because I love that kind of stuff!

APPENDIX

The goal of this book is to help you design the training plan that will be tailored to you and your needs to enable you to prepare for your race.

I've done my best to explain every nuance of my process for working with my clients to help them train for their races in the best way possible for them.

You have in your hands all of the information that you need to create your training plan. But if you're like me, there are times when a picture is worth more than a thousand words.

With that said, I'd like to share with you a few examples of actual training plans that I've created for some of my clients.

Each example is unique, obviously, so looking through them may help you visualize how you want to structure your training with days off, how to space out your workouts, and how best to bump up your mileage over the course of your training.

Use them for inspiration. Use them as guides.

Just don't use them as they are, because they aren't for you.

Got it?

I created the following training plan for a client that already had a solid base of fitness coming into the start of the training cycle. This client had been running 5+ days per week for many months leading up to the start of the training plan, in addition to doing regular strength training.

Tip: I have added this plan as a download in the resources section so you can read it more clearly. These images are to give you an idea.

June 2016						
Sunday	Monday	Tuesday	Wednesday	Thursday	Friday	Saturday
29	30 Memorial Day	31	1	2	3	4
5	6	7	8	9	10	11
12 Long Run 14 Miles	13 Strength	14 Easy Run 60 Min	15 Hard Run Tempo Run 1+ Mile Warm Up 4 Miles @ Tempo Pace (15-30 sec slower than 5k Pace) 1 Mile Cool Down	16 Strength	17 Easy Run 60 Min	18 Long Run 14-15 Miles All Easy
19 Father's Day Off Day Enjoy the Hub's Race. Cheer Loud!	20 Strength	21 Easy Run 60 Min	22 Hard Run Long Repeats 1+ Mile Warm Up 4x1 mile w/ .5 mile walk/jog recovery 1 Mile Cool Down	23 Strength	24 Easy Run 60 Min	25 Easy Run 3-4 Miles Easy
26 Long Run 15+ Miles 5 Easy, 5 MP, 5 Easy	27 Strength Vegas	28 Easy Run 60 Min Vegas	29 Hard Run Wild Card Choose your own adventure based on what you can do in Vegas. Vegas	30 Strength Vegas	1	2
3	4 Independence Day	Notes				

Calendar Templates by Vertex42.com
http://www.vertex42.com/calendars/
© 2013 Vertex42 LLC. free to print.

2016 Calendars   2012 Calendars

July 2016

June '16
S M T W T F S

August '16
S M T W T F S

September '16
S M T W T F S

Sunday	Monday	Tuesday	Wednesday	Thursday	Friday	Saturday
26	27	28	29	30	1 **Canada Day 5k** Have Fun!	2 **Off Day**
3 **Long Run** 12-13 Miles All Easy Ended up w/ 16 #overachiever	4 **Strength**	5 **Easy Run** 60 Min	6 **Hard Run** 2 Mile Repeats 1+ Mile Warm Up 2x2 mile w/ .5 mile walk/jog recovery 1 Mile Cool Down	7 **Strength**	8 **Easy Run** 60 Min	9 **Easy Run** 3-4 Miles Easy
10 **Long Run** 15 Miles Total 5 Easy, 5 MP, 5 Easy	11 **Strength**	12 **Easy Run** 60 Min	13 **Hard Run** 2 Mile Repeats 1+ Mile Warm Up 2x2 mile w/ .5 mile walk/jog recovery 1 Mile Cool Down	14 **Strength**	15 **Easy Run** 60 Min (30-40 Min if Running Saturday)	16 **Off Day** RESPECT THE OFF DAY! Especially with two long runs next week!
17 **Long Run** Negative Split 16 Miles Goals: First 8 Miles: 9:30-9:45 Pace (76-78 Min) Last 8 Miles: 9:00-9:15 Pace (72-74 Min)	18 **Strength**	19 **Easy Run** 60 Min	20 **Hard Run** Tempo Run 1+ Mile Warm Up 5 Miles @ Tempo Pace (15-30 sec slower than 5k Pace) 1 Mile Cool Down	21 **Strength**	22 **Long Run** 15-17 Miles All Easy	23 Vacation-No Running
24 Vacation-No Running	25 Vacation-No Running	26 Vacation-No Running	27 Vacation-No Running	28 Vacation-No Running	29 Vacation-No Running	30 **Easy Run** 3-4 Miles Easy
31 **Long Run** 16-18 Miles All Easy	1	Notes				

Calendar Templates by Vertex42.com
http://www.vertex42.com/calendars/
© 2013 Vertex42 LLC. How to print.

2016 Calendars   2017 Calendars

133

August 2016

Sunday	Monday	Tuesday	Wednesday	Thursday	Friday	Saturday
31 Long Run 16-18 Miles All Easy	**1** Strength	**2** Easy Run 60 Min	**3** Hard Run Mile Repeats 1+ Mile Warm Up 4x1 mile w/ .5 mile walk/jog recovery 1 Mile Cool Down	**4** Strength	**5** Easy Run 60 Min	**6** Easy Run 3-4 Miles Easy
7 Long Run 17 Miles Total 5 Easy, 7 @ MP, 5 Easy	**8** Strength	**9** Easy Run 60-90 Min	**10** Hard Run 2 Mile Repeats 1+ Mile Warm Up 2x2 mile w/ .5 mile walk/jog recovery 1 Mile Cool Down	**11** Strength	**12** Easy Run 60-90 Min	**13** Off Day
14 Long Run 19-20 Miles Negative Split	**15** Strength	**16** Easy Run 60-90 Min	**17** Hard Run Tempo Run 1+ Mile Warm Up 5 Miles @ Tempo Pace (15-30 sec slower than 5k Pace) 1 Mile Cool Down	**18** Strength	**19** Easy Run 60-90 Min	**20** Easy Run 3-4 Miles Easy
21 Long Run 20-22+ Miles All Easy	**22** Strength	**23** Easy Run 60-90 Min	**24** Hard Run 1/2 Mile Repeats 1+ Mile Warm Up 8x800m w/ 400m Recovery Balls to the Walls for the 8s Cool Down	**25** Strength	**26** Easy Run 60-90 Min	**27** Off Day
28 Long Run 20+ Miles 5 Easy, 10 @ MP, 5+ Easy	**29** Strength	**30** Easy Run 60-90 Min	**31** Hard Run Speed-ish 1+ Mile Warm Up 2 Hard/.5 Recovery 2x1 Mile Hard/.5 Rec Cool Down	**1**	**2**	**3**
4	**5** Labor Day	Notes				

October 2016

Sunday	Monday	Tuesday	Wednesday	Thursday	Friday	Saturday
25	26	27	28	29	30	1 Off Day
2 Long Run 10-13 Miles All Easy	3 Strength	4 Easy Run 60 Min Max	5 Hard Run 1+ Mile Warm Up 3 Miles @ Tempo Pace (15-30 sec slower than 5k Pace) 1 Mile Cool Down	6 Off Day	7 Off Day This is the day we will be driving the 7 hrs to Minneapolis	8 Easy Run Shakeout 2-4 Miles Easy
9 Race Day Twin Cities Marathon: Give Em Hell!	10 Off Day	11 Off Day	12 Off Day Foam Rolling/Stretching OK Non-Impact Cardio (easy) OK	13 Off Day Foam Rolling/Stretching OK Non-Impact Cardio (easy) OK	14 Off Day Foam Rolling/Stretching OK Non-Impact Cardio (easy) OK	15 Off Day Foam Rolling/Stretching OK Non-Impact Cardio (easy) OK
16 Off Day Foam Rolling/Stretching OK Non-Impact Cardio (easy) OK	17 Strength Easy Strength Training	18 Off Day Foam Rolling/Stretching OK Non-Impact Cardio (easy) OK	19 Easy Run* Only if Legs Feel 100% 30 Min Max	20 Off Day Foam Rolling/Stretching OK Non-Impact Cardio (easy) OK	21 Strength Easy Strength Training	22 Easy Run* Only if Legs Feel 100% 45 Min Max
23	24	25	26	27	28	29
30	31 Halloween	Notes				

Calendar Templates by Vertex42.com
http://www.vertex42.com/calendars/
© 2013 Vertex42 LLC. Free to print.
2016 Calendars   2017 Calendars

135

September 2016

Sunday	Monday	Tuesday	Wednesday	Thursday	Friday	Saturday
28	29	30	31	1 Strength	2 Easy Run 60-90 Min	3 Easy Run 3-4 Miles Easy
4 Long Run 15-16 Miles	5 Labor Day Strength gym closed - will be a run day 60-90 Min	6 Easy Run Gym open - will be a strength day	7 Hard Run Tempo Run 1+ Mile Warm Up 3 Miles @ Tempo Pace (15-30 sec slower than 5k Pace) 1 Mile Cool Down	8 Strength	9 Easy Run 60-90 Min	10 Off Day
11 Race Day Local 30k TC Tune Up	12 Strength	13 Easy Run 60 Min Max Easy	14 Hard Run 1+ Mile Warm Up 3-4 Miles @ 8:30ish 1 Mile Cool Down	15 Strength	16 Easy Run 60-90 Min	17 Easy Run 3-4 Miles Easy
18 Long Run 15-17 All Easy	19 Strength	20 Easy Run 60-90 Min	21 Hard Run Mile Repeats 1+ Mile Warm Up 4x1 mile w/ .5 mile walk/jog recovery 1 Mile Cool Down	22 Strength	23 Easy Run 60-90 Min	24 Off Day
25 Long Run 20-22 Miles 5 Easy, 10 @ MP, 5+ Easy	26 Strength	27 Easy Run 60-90 Min	28 Hard Run 1+ Mile Warm Up 2 Hard/.5 Recovery 1 Mile Hard Cool Down	29 Strength	30 Easy Run 60-90 Min	1
2	3 Rosh Hashanah	Notes				

A few things to note from this plan:

The dedication to strength training throughout the plan

Two days per week, every week, until the week before the race.

Most runs were easy

Even for this runner with a solid base of fitness already in place, the commitment to doing easy miles was essential. One hard workout per week + regularly adding hard miles to the long run provided the right balance of hard and easy miles.

The number of really long runs

In this case, the heavy volume of mileage was completely warranted. This runner wanted to work on feeling strong beyond 20 miles, so we did several runs of 20+ miles in preparation for going 26.2 miles on race day following the "finish line is in sight" strategy.

Additional examples of training plans, as well as areas of note for each plan, are included with the downloadable bonuses included with this book.

See the resource page for details.

▍RESOURCES

I have created several resources/tools/bonuses that you, as a reader of this book, can use to help you write your training plan successfully.

FREE DOWNLOADS

I want you to be successful, and as such I want you to have all the tools that you need to put your plan together, including:

- The self-assessment of current fitness form.
- Your weekly running availability chart.
- Five most overlooked exercises for runners guide.
- The sample plan in the appendix.
- Actual training plans created for and used by my clients to act as visual examples for you as you create your training plan.

Head to the link below, download the resources, and use them!

DizRuns.com/brordextras

NEED A HAND

I get it, writing a comprehensive training plan is a little more involved than it seems.

Relax.

You know what you're doing, and I know that you'll figure it out.

That said, if you'd like to jump on the phone/Skype for some help working through whatever trouble spot you're facing at the moment, I'm here for you.

Just head to DizRuns.com/consultation and schedule a call.

Want to get a consultation call for free?

Head over to Amazon and write a review for the book, take a screenshot of your review, send it to me (diz@dizruns.com), and your first consultation call is on me.

NEED MORE THAN A HAND

You can totally write your training plan, but do you even want to?

If you'd rather focus on simply doing the workouts instead of writing the entire training plan, I'm happy to work with you to help you make sure you'll be ready on race day.

Check out the different coaching options that I have available, and find the one that is right for you, at DizRuns.com/coaching.

KEEP IN TOUCH

Don't be a stranger, eh?

Come over and join our Facebook group, and you can hang out and compare training notes with hundreds of other runners from around the world.

As long as you don't mind cracking a few jokes and simply nerding out on our sport, we'd love to have you join us.

DizRuns.com/Facebook

TWITTER, INSTAGRAM AND BEYOND

I'm a sucker for social media, and I've been known to jump on any/every platform around to check it out.

And when I do, the handle is always the same: @dizruns.

At the time of writing this book, Instagram and Twitter are my jam. I would love it if you'd connect with me on either platform.

And whatever the new social media thing is in the future, there's a good chance I'll be there as well. So say hi, ok?

EMAIL WORKS TOO

No matter what the future holds for social media, I can't see email disappearing.

Feel free to drop me an email anytime and let me know how you're doing with writing your training plan and let me know how your race went.

Or just say hey and we can shoot the breeze.

Have a great training cycle and a better race,

Denny

diz@dizruns.com

YOU KNOW IT, NOW DO IT!

Seriously.

Stop reading. Start writing your plan. Now.

19508151R00085